GOD'S PASSION,
OUR PASSION

GOD'S PASSION, OUR PASSION

The Only Way to Love ... Every Day

PIERRE WOLFF

Translated by Carol Eggers

TRIUMPH™ BOOKS
Liguori, Missouri

Published by Triumph™ Books
Liguori, Missouri
An Imprint of Liguori Publications

Most of the scriptural citations are from:

The New American Bible, copyright © 1970 by the Confraternity of Christian Doctrine, Washington, D.C., and are used with permission. All rights reserved.

The Jerusalem Bible by Alexander Jones, ed., copyright © 1966 by Darton, Longman & Todd, Ltd. and Doubleday, a division of Bantam Doubleday Dell Publishing Group, Inc., and used by permission of Doubleday, a division of Bantam Doubleday Dell Publishing Group, Inc.

The Catholic Study Bible, The New American Bible, by Oxford University Press, Inc., New York, copyright © 1990 by Oxford University Press, Inc., and used by permission of Oxford University Press, Inc.

Library of Congress Cataloging-in-Publication Data

Wolff, Pierre, 1929–
    God's passion, our passion : the only way to love...every day /
Pierre Wolff : translated by Carol Eggers. — 1st ed.
      p. cm.
    Includes bibliographical references and index.
    ISBN 0-89243-641-7 : $9.95
    1. Jesus Christ—Passion. 2. Spiritual life. 3. Love—Religious
aspects—Christianity.   I. Title.
    BT431.W65   1994
    232.96–dc20   93-36056
                                                            CIP

To my brother, Raymond (1923–1992)

To my wife, Mary

Contents

Preface

I WOULD LIKE TO MAKE a few promises to my readers about what they can hope to get out of this book, whether or not they happen to be Christian. The account of the Passion-Resurrection of Jesus is the longest part of the Gospels and was the first one preached in the original communities that gave birth to Christianity, because it was important. Though Christians often spend relatively little time with these pages in their celebrations or in their private prayer, the revelation of these texts is undeniable for them, as well as for anyone who has been influenced by Christian culture.

For those who have felt the cultural impact of Christianity, the message of Jesus, in the sense that the primitive Church understood it, remains essential. It expresses in an unprecedented way what is precious to many people: love. So for anyone who has been influenced by Christian culture, the notion of love depends on what Jesus says to us about love in his Passion. For example, the Declaration of the Human Rights of the U.N. (1948), which describes the dignity of human beings, was supervised by the five major powers of that time; the representatives of four of those nations were under the Christian sphere of influence. Movements like the Red Cross or Amnesty International were also born in a Christian environment; their care for suffering people depends on their roots. When we talk about human dignity and care for human be-

ings, we are not far from the narratives of the Passion. Of
course, this is even more evident for Christians. So my
hope is that reading this book will deepen their knowledge
of love.

More specifically, I promise a rich harvest for many
Christian groups. Preachers can find material for their sermons. Teachers of the Christian faith may be able to
use many themes for classes, days of reflection or prayer.
Spiritual helpers can draw criteria from these pages for
discernment with those they are accompanying. Liturgists
will employ some of these ideas to develop certain aspects
of the Passion in their celebrations (an example: It is possible to insert a penitential rite in a talk inspired by the
chapter "Ecce Homo.")

And to those who are suffering, what can this book
promise? To the extent that a book can help them at a
painful time, I think that this one will permit them to
discover more clearly how Jesus, in his Passion, is their
brother, and how his God is more present to them than
they think and does not answer their questions as the God
of Job did. I would like to thank here all those who have allowed me to share in their Passions. They became for me
the immediate presence of all the Passions of the world.
They taught me to read Jesus' Passion, and he taught me
to read theirs. In passing, I thank Carol who helped me to
find the right words.

But the most important promise is deeper than all of
that. Some preachers treat the Passion as an opportunity to
talk about our sins. It is true that the accounts of Jesus' ordeal help us to do that — and I won't overlook this point in
this book. However, I don't think that Jesus revealed very
much concerning our sinfulness. As a nonbeliever said to
me, "I really don't need your Christian revelation to see
that humankind has always made mistakes that are ter-
ribly detrimental for everybody." The disciples also knew
that, through their own experience and through the reading of the Old Testament. So if they were surprised by

Jesus' words and actions, it was not principally by the revelation of sin.

Jesus, in his Passion, brought us something deeper we can all discover, something that "has lain hidden from the foundation of the world" (Mt 13:35). He is the Lamb, the only one "worthy... to receive the scroll and break open its seals," worthy to tell us who is God (Rv 5:9). By pondering these pages and using them as a help for prayer, Christians will be able to see through Jesus the beauty of their God revealed in an extraordinary way in the Passion. It is there that Jesus' prayer is heard, "That they should know you, *the only true God*," that his assertion is perfectly true, "Whoever has seen me has seen the Father" (Jn 17:3; 14:9). The God seen in the man of Nazareth is a love sometimes difficult to accept, but one not really foreign to our experience.

Any love, any friendship, and any service is this God acting in the human heart. That is why these pages will always connect the Passion of Jesus to our daily experiences with our family or friends, in our society, and as a nation among nations. But they will also remain faithful to the desire of Jesus, to the extent that we can perceive it, to recall and reveal more deeply to his contemporaries who God is. For if God is Love, and Love within us by the Spirit, then to say something about God and about human relationships is to talk about the same mystery. The Passion of God can only be ours; it is our Passion.

Introduction

I HAVE ALWAYS BEEN IMPRESSED by the impact that Holy Week has on Christians. This can be illustrated by what happened one time when I was working with someone who had come to me for spiritual help. She had begun praying with Luke's Gospel and was meditating on Jesus' birth. At precisely that time the Church was celebrating Holy Week, and she attended the services in her parish. When these rituals were over, she could not go back to the crib: The experience of Holy Week had made too great an impression on her. But why should this surprise us? *Holy* Week is not just a week like any other week. If we remember that the word "holy" in the Old Testament means "apart," this week is in a class of its own because it is extra-ordinary: Something distinguishes this week from the other weeks of the year. What?

Let's not answer this question too quickly, because we might take for granted what these days are telling us and miss their richness. We might gather only the most obvious and superficial fruit from the events narrated there. We could, for example, let ourselves get too taken up with the physical sufferings of Jesus (when many people in history have suffered an even more atrocious martyrdom). In this week there is something that should surprise us, amaze us.

The first thing that surprises us is the very length of the Passion narrative in all Gospels. This segment is longer than the part that describes the Resurrection, for instance, even though this mystery is the focal point of Christian

1

faith. The depiction of a mere sixty hours in Jesus' life is also extremely long when compared to the account of his whole public life, which scholars think may have lasted about three years. Why should so much space be occupied by such a brief event? If we accept that the text of Mark was one of the first ones written, can we assume that the first Christians who read his words needed a more detailed account than those who heard the story from John years later? It might be that closeness in time to a death makes it more present and leads us to be more curious about the details of the event than would be the case if some time had passed. If we add to this what the exegetes have told us, that the first preaching by the disciples (and hence the first writings) concerned mainly the Passion and the Resurrection of Jesus, then we must admit that to narrate, commentate, explain, and perhaps justify the Passion (and the Resurrection) was a pressing need for these early announcers of the Good News.

If that is the way it was, it's probably because there were in the disciples' minds (as well as in those who were interested in this new religion) many questions born of a very painful shock. We can surmise that the first Christians questioned this end of Jesus, which could only have been seen as a colossal failure. Maybe also they were looking for an explanation in his death of the death of their martyrs, since persecution was not long in coming. It's obvious in the story of Stephen's stoning that the faithful drew a parallel with Jesus' death (Acts 6–7; 5:17ff). And like the early Church, we too can find equivalents to the Passion and its question, about God this time, in our own lives.

We can certainly find echoes of this in our own experience. Recall your own reaction when the news of a brutal and unexpected death reached you: the sudden loss of a child, for example, or the assassination of a charismatic leader. As always, death is a shock, but *that* death was an outrage! Didn't you wonder, even say, "Why did God let that happen?" And if some ill-advised preacher said,

"It's God's will," your indignation only grew! I remember the offense that we felt, some friends and I, when a church leader dared to preach to us about the "mystery of God's will" after a tidal wave had killed a million people in Bangladesh! We see that the Passion is already upon us in our own drama when we dare to ask, "What kind of God is behind such a tragedy?" "Unknown God" maybe (Acts 17:23; 1 Cor 2:9)? And that's just what must have been going on in the minds and hearts of the first Christians. To be crucified in those days was the equivalent of being sent to the electric chair. That someone like Jesus, who claimed to be on such intimate terms with God, could die that kind of death could only be an outrage, a scandal for his disciples. They had to talk about it, think about it, contemplate and ruminate in order to comprehend that the God hidden and revealed in the Passion of Jesus was not the God they imagined — is not the God that most of us still imagine.

So now let us enter into the Passion, but allowing ourselves to be surprised — to be amazed. May the text act for us as Philip did with the court official of Candace reading Isaiah 53:7–8 without understanding the verses about "the sheep led to the slaughter...the lamb before the shearer." May it reveal to us "the Good News, Jesus," and his God (Acts 8:32–35). I will start by describing some general trends of the Passion as a whole; then I will enter into greater detail, following the chronology of the events.

Passion

THE FACT THAT THE EVENTS of the Passion (and the Resurrection) were the first to be preached, and written about, tells us something else: For the first disciples they were the most important events of Jesus' life, and therefore of their own lives. We can guess that what went on during those three days appeared quite quickly to Christians to be the heart of the new revelation. This would suggest that if, today, we had only the texts that describe those hours, that would be sufficient for our faith, for knowing everything about our relationship with God and who the God of Jesus Christ is. In fact, we can start by letting ourselves be amazed by one word, the one frequently used to summarize all that happened, the word "passion."

In the context of the Christian liturgy, the word signifies sufferings, dereliction, and death. It implies everything that Jesus experienced during those days: betrayal and denial, rejection and abandonment, and other ordeals. The word "passion" in this context suggests little that is pleasant for a human being. We often forget that we use it as an adjective when we speak of a passionate love. This time the word has a very positive connotation: It means that what we describe is pushed to its very limits, to its fulfillment. When we see a passionate love, we sometimes talk about the madness of love.

That is what the Passion of Jesus Christ is about. As Christians, don't we see in these events a passion-tide of love in human flesh, the crashing waves of the God called

Love by John (1 Jn 4:8)? So when we read or pray the Passion narrative, we listen to a love story — not a romance, but the story of God's love for us, the story of God as Love.

If anyone asks us to define love, we say that to love is to give. Without a doubt this is a part of love, and the Passion speaks about this aspect of love in Jesus and in the God he reveals. During his public life, Jesus certainly gave: The Gospels show us Jesus giving to eat and drink, giving his time and his care, his teaching and forgiveness; and, in the end — and here, we enter into the Passion — giving what he calls his flesh and blood under the form of bread and wine. Several hours later, on the cross, he gives his mother and finally his life. This tells us how much the God of Jesus has given us and wants to.

But also the Passion introduces another dimension of love, one that we know but easily forget. As long as my love for you is essentially "giving," I control the process. I decide the gift, its size, and how and when it will be given. You are free to accept it or refuse it, but that is the only part of this transaction that belongs to you. Everything else is in my hands and subject to the decision of my will. If I give you this gift it can probably be said that I love you, but in a hidden way I am still the master of the action and this leaves room for being proud of my generosity. Maybe if I loved you more deeply, I would hand over what always lies behind the giving of gifts: power. My love for you moves to another level if, while continuing to give to you, I begin giving myself up to you. I am still the subject of the action, for I initiate it, but I don't finish it. As soon as I abandon myself into your hands, you become the master of the situation and you can do whatever you want. Power has changed hands because I have handed it over to you. This time I love you right to the end, because I give you everything, including power over my very liberty. I am yours.

Here's what we see in Jesus' Passion, and the evangelists did not miss this point. Within the narrative of the three days the expression "handed over" is repeated forty-

one times. It suggests a package that changes hands, and
without much thought. The people who arrest Jesus hand
him over to Caiaphas; Caiaphas hands him over to his
servants, who play games with him, then on to Pilate; Pilate hands him over to soldiers, who deliver him to his
executioners. When you count up all these hand-to-hand
exchanges, you come out with eight (including Annas and
Herod in John and Luke). And each time the delivery was
not made carefully; after all, he was just a prisoner. In fact,
what happens to Jesus is not that surprising. He ends his
life the way he started it. In Bethlehem, Jesus was already
handed over to anyone who came by, because he was a
baby. The God who we see in Jesus appears to us, from the
beginning until the end, as a God who is given to us to the
point of complete abandonment! God, Love, in our hands.

We can do with Love whatever we want. Our love, Love
in us — if we believe in the Spirit's presence in us — is at
our mercy. We can subject our love to the best or the worst
of treatment. We can give love in us and around us the
possibility of existing fully, of growing and bearing fruit,
of spreading for our joy and the joy of all around us. We
can also wound, damage, and kill the love that is in us and
around us, to the great detriment of all, starting with ourselves. When we are face to face with the Passion of God in
Jesus, we have to face our behavior toward Love as well.

The narrative interrogates us, "What have you done,
what are you doing with the love that is in you or surrounds you?" This question addresses our attempts to run
away, to absent ourselves, to abandon and deny, to betray
and condemn, to wound and to kill. But the story reminds us also of the times when we have given or handed
ourselves over, been present in a helping way, sustained
or supported, remained faithful and full of understanding,
bandaged up and saved someone's life. The Passion of God
and the Passion of Jesus of two thousand years ago? The
Passion of Love in each one of us today? Both. The Passion
is our Passion.

Is This God the One
We Believe In?

"SO THIS SLAUGHTER of an innocent man was a love story? You must be kidding," some people might say. If it is true, the Passion is a huge paradox unfortunately repeated in all the parodies of justice that history has seen too often. There's another general direction in the Gospels that only accentuates this impression of paradox.

When we examine the four Gospels, the differences in the way they handle the Passion are striking — for example, between Mark and John. John portrays a Jesus passing through his trial like a larger-than-life hero, moving fearlessly toward a fate decreed by dwarfs. This is obvious when he talks with Pilate on equal terms. Pilate was the symbol of the Roman Empire. Even though we are talking about something that happened two thousand years ago, it is still quite extraordinary that a little no-account preacher dares to confront such a powerful man. A similar situation today might be Nelson Mandela confronting the government of South Africa for the first time, after years of imprisonment. Yes, Jesus' enemies direct the situation, but in John he is the one who is in control. John wrote after years of pondering this mysterious Jesus and wanted to emphasize his divinity.

Mark's approach is totally different. He is very precise and enters into some details; his style is fairly dry. He writes like a news reporter who gives only the facts without editorializing. We don't find many references to the Old Testament, for example, used to explain and justify the events — as we do in Matthew. There are no scenes that soften the horror of the ordeal, while Luke has a consoling angel and a cure, Pilate's self-doubt and women who weep over Jesus, and eventually a kind-hearted thief, as if to spread a little soothing salve on a painful wound (22:43, 51; 23:13–16, 20, 28, 39–43). Mark gives us the facts in all their naked brutality. The Lord of the Passion of John does not show up in Mark's account. Mark seems to say to us, "Look, here are the facts; you figure it out." But how can we deal with this? Everything turns out completely different from what we were expecting. We have nothing but a paradox.

Mark began by showing us Jesus as the "Son of God" (1:1). We might expect that such a person, after all the good he did during his lifetime, would be publicly acclaimed. But he becomes a laughingstock. Turned in for a pittance, he is betrayed, denied, and abandoned; they choose a criminal over him (14:10, 30–31, 66ff; 15:11). They take him so easily for an outlaw that everybody — high priests, scribes, onlookers, and even the two other men crucified with him — insults him (15:29–32). The ease with which all of this happens is underscored by Mark's clipped and blunt style. To top it all off, Jesus calls himself, "The Son of Man seated at the right hand of the Power!" The noteworthy and sophisticated members of the Sanhedrin are completely shocked, and they knock him around, ignobly, treating him like less than a servant (15:29–32).

The whole thing would be a complete farce, if it weren't so tragic. There have been a lot of farces of this kind in the annals of prisons and concentration camps. But if we remember, didn't this all start in grammar school when we made fun of a smaller or a handicapped child or a classmate with a different color skin or with a different background? How about when that big kid, the one we

were really afraid of, tripped and fell on his face and we all
stood around laughing and hooting? The revenge of cowards and mean-spirited people when they have nothing to
lose is something we can all understand. How many great
minds, catered to in their day, have been left in the dust
once political, ideological, or spiritual power excommunicated them? Mark's account is close to our daily life.

We must admit we were looking for a strong Jesus.
Mark himself describes his power over adversaries, disease,
nature, and even demons; but here, in his Passion, he is
extremely weak. He begs his disciples to stay beside him
in the olive grove; he does nothing when the soldiers come
for him, and there he cures nobody (14:33)! It is as if his
power as a miracle worker deserts him (14:47). He says absolutely nothing (14:55–59; 15:5). The strong one is made
a fool of by servants (14:65). The absurdity of it all becomes clear when we recall that the Just One is going to
be killed over a mere matter of jealousy (15:10)!

When someone that strong becomes this weak, it's no
surprise to see his disciples desert him. That the important people are against him can be easily explained, and
we have known about that since chapter 2 (2:6). But when
even his disciples leave him, that's a surprise. Let's give
them the benefit of the doubt: Isn't this too much of a
paradox? They are half asleep and they don't know what
to say (14:10). And if they still follow him, it is at a distance, like Peter (14:54). The paradox is so complete that
they can't "follow." Their certainty about Jesus crumbles
because he does. He did not measure up to their expectations, and in one line, in two words really, it is all over.
"Crucify him!" — that's all there is.

It is all there, if we understand Mark's paradox. But we
don't understand unless we realize that our expectations,
deceived and disappointed, are surprised by a revelation we
are not ready for. Mark makes us say, as Jacob did, "Truly,
the Lord is in this spot, although I did not know it!" (Gn
28:16). In Jesus a God is revealed who does not match our

usual notion of God. Before this God, like the disciples, we don't know what to say, and we don't even know what is being said to us (14:40; 15:34). We are shocked like Pilate and outraged like the apostles (15:5, 44; 14:27). Because this God of the Passion, this Love, is Someone we don't know — especially if we think about our current conception of God and love. If we put aside for a moment the fact that we know how the story turned out, Mark artfully arranges many surprises for us. The disciples are surprised at Mary's waste of perfume, Judas' betrayal, and Jesus' fear. They are surprised at a death sentence that is handed down in spite of witnesses who can't even agree among themselves; they are surprised by Jesus' silence. The final surprise comes when he dies: It's not his companions who say, "Truly this man was God's son"; it's a pagan!

But when the Temple curtain is torn in two and the Holy of Holies is exposed, we see God unveiled. We see a void, because there was no image of God in that place. Mark's paradox ends with a God who voids *all our usual representations of divinity*, just as the Crucified One cancels out the image that the disciples had of the expected Messiah. Mark is the only evangelist who maintains this perspective right to the end. His text ends in 16:8, leaving us with the women "bewildered and trembling," seized by "great fear" after seeing an empty tomb, and "a young man in brilliant garb," who said that Jesus was alive (16:2–8).

So while reading Mark, we face some questions. When we say "God," what do we have in mind? What do we mean by "God is Love"? And what do we expect in our love relationships? Don't we usually have in our minds a notion that is quite far from the Gospel revelation?

Mark shows us Jesus covered with a veil by those who deride him (14:65). This reminds us of Moses coming back from Mount Sinai after "he had conversed with the Lord." "The skin of his face had become radiant," and after he had finished speaking with the Israelites, "he put a veil over his face." He hid the brightness of the Glory of God

that shone in his face (Ex 34:29–35). Jesus said what he
had to say, did what he had to do during his public life, and
now a veil covers his face, because the new glory of God
shines on him and through him — the new Moses bringing
the new covenant (2 Cor 4:6). But it is shining so brightly
that we are blinded, because it was, it is, the glory of a
God different from what we are used to seeing. Instead of
some of our images of God that are many times a mockery of God, Mark gives us a God who is a Love turning
everything upside down.

Beauty Destroyed, Beauty Revealed *

THROUGH THE PASSION we see Jesus' beauty progressively, inexorably destroyed. When we behold him on the cross, he has already endured hours of interrogation, insults, and torture, hours of loneliness without comfort or support. He has been totally disfigured. The words of Isaiah are not too strong:

> Even as many were amazed at him — so marred was his look beyond that of a man, and his appearance beyond that of mortals.... He grew up like a sapling before [the Lord,] like a shoot from the parched earth; there was in him no stately bearing to make us look at him, nor appearance that would attract us to him. He was spurned and avoided by men, a man of suffering, accustomed to infirmity. One of those from whom men hide their faces, spurned, and we held him in no esteem. (Is 52:13–53:12)

Hatred and fear are operating so clearly in the Passion narrative that it seems that an evil machine has been turned on and cannot be stopped. Each event seems inevitable, and a certain face of God is destroyed in Jesus. His enemies set out to deliberately destroy him piece by piece. Is this as unfamiliar as we think? We have to look

---

*Is 52:13–53:12; Wis 2:10–20.

at children to see it: Sometimes they deliberately destroy
their toys; they must find out what's inside them, what
they are made of. They don't stop until the pieces are
scattered all over the floor.

We did the same thing with our parents when we were
adolescents. We assaulted them with confrontations and
attacks. Maybe we didn't want to destroy them, but we certainly wanted to find out what they had inside them. We
tested them. Our parents were often torn apart by the feelings that were provoked by this sort of crucifixion. They
were forced to learn and to demonstrate how much they
could absorb and endure of suffering. They were forced to
show themselves and their torturers the quality of the love
that dwelt within them. "Let us see if what he says is true.
... Let us test him with cruelty and with torture, and thus
explore this gentleness of his and put his endurance to the
proof," says the book of Wisdom, portraying the words of
those who were hounding the just person (Wis 2:17, 19).
These lines hit home. This happens in our own trials as
well as in the Passion of Jesus.

Judith had said, "God is not a man that he should be
moved by threats, nor human, that he may be given an
ultimatum" (Jdt 8:16). But I see the Passion as a test created by humanity for the God announced by Christ. The
end result is that, even though a certain *image* of God was
slowly destroyed in Jesus while he was undergoing torture,
a truth was being revealed as well: who God really is. What
kind of God is the God of Jesus Christ? This is not foreign
to us. Some sorrowful passions eventually reveal truth.

*Two people are divorcing. But the process reveals the
quality of love they have been sharing. The conscious
or unconscious selfishness that slowly snuffed out the
love they had at the beginning is laid bare: She was
more a mother than a wife; he wanted a servant
rather than an equal partner; she got married to escape her parents; he was really married to his work.*

A devastating storm erupts in a family between parents and children, because of drugs, alcoholism, or the unexpected pregnancy of one daughter. The stress reveals whether or not the bonds that unite them are authentic and profound on both sides.

Employee-management relations are tested by economic hard times, and the question of a strike splits the workers into factions. But the conflict reveals the underlying interests of all parties.

Under the relentless light of a crisis our deepest values are clearly revealed. The revelation is even clearer when the focal point is someone who stands for justice, who represents a "cause." This person becomes a target for everyone who is disturbed by the message she/he proclaims. Deep down, when our own false gods are denounced — in our family, neighborhood, firm, or nation — don't we repeat the words of Wisdom:

Let us lie in wait for the virtuous man, since he annoys us and opposes our way of life, reproaches us for our breaches of the law and accuses us of playing false to our upbringing. . . . Before us he stands like the censure of our thoughts; the very sight of him weighs our spirits down; his way of life is not like others', the paths he treads are unfamiliar. In his opinion we are counterfeit; he holds aloof from our doings as though from filth." (Wis 2:12, 14–16)

We may have spread rumors and gossip, made underhanded insinuations, and, sometimes, directly attacked when somebody dared to question the gods we were adoring. Have we been a part of the Passion when those who blew the whistle on racism, social injustice, or professional malpractice, when those who denounced the political oppression or exploitation of the poor were calumniated?

In the paradoxical scandal of the cross, all of our idolatry was revealed. The way we idolize social classes and status is reflected in Pilate. Our worship of power is made visible in the priests, scribes, and elders of the Sanhedrin. The cult we have of the law and of our self-righteousness is prefigured in the Pharisees. The way we genuflect before our wallets and bow before our vision of achievement is symbolized by Judas. The homage we pay to our precious lives is seen in the disciples' lack of courage. Clearly, we have been "there"!

The words of Wisdom can be easily put into the mouths of the ones who destroyed Jesus:

> He claims to have knowledge of God and calls himself a son of the Lord.... He proclaims the final end of the virtuous as happy and boasts of having God for his father. Let us see if what he says is true, let us observe what kind of end he himself will have. If the virtuous man is God's son, God will take his part and rescue him from the clutches of his enemies." (Wis 2:13, 16–18)

But this same text goes on to say, "They do not know the hidden things of God" (2:22).

These people tried to protect themselves with their gods; so do we. Jesus is the obstacle in their way; so he must be destroyed. But they became the engineers of a revelation that God wanted to make to us (Ps 33:10–11). In fact, they prepared the best way — even though it was an atrocity — for allowing the desire of God to be manifested without ambiguities. For looking at God crucified, we have to say, "Really, God is not like all our idols!"

I don't know what children find when they dismantle their toys. But I do know the loving forgiveness I discovered when, as an adolescent, I tried to take my mother apart. When we defend our idols and false images of God, we disfigure and destroy in ourselves and for others the authentic God whose witnesses we are supposed to be. Who has not been tempted to reject God because of the teaching of the first catechists we met in our family, at school, or in our parish? Atheism has won out in many countries because the Churches have not always announced and shown in their deeds the God of Jesus Christ. The wars between Christian denominations, the compromise of the Churches' leaders with political power and money, a compassionless clerical authoritarianism have been a terrible way of the cross for God in human history.

But God survived, thanks to true witnesses of the Gospel who were sometimes martyrs, or even victims of their own Church. In fact, God's image has often been purified of many counterfeits during these historical Passions. For at the very moment that the visible beauty of Jesus was being effaced, the real beauty of God — invisible often because we are so near-sighted — was appearing. In the Crucified, we see a God who is not a power God, not a thunder and lightning storm, neither a hurricane nor an earthquake. This God is not a burning and devouring forest fire. Instead we hear the "whisper" of a God who is the "gentle breeze" of Love, like the prophet Elijah understood when all the powers of the kingdom of Israel were against him (1 Kgs 19).

The Crucified One reveals a God to us who is *other* than all our gods, an incredible Love beyond all our definitions, images, and hopes. Our personal experiences, like the ones described earlier, can help us to understand if not who God is, then that a Love like this is so enormous that our hearts will never be disappointed. We expected a gallon of water only, so we tested God in the crucifixion. And from Jesus' pierced side, an ocean was revealed and given to us: Love, totally Other, fathomless. Perhaps that's why some Christians, before the rather ugly picture of the Crucified One, do not feel horrified. They feel invited to give thanks, amazed before such a Love-God. Each of the scenes of the Passion will only unfold the facets of the revelation of this Beauty.

*Priceless**

T HE PEOPLE INVOLVED DIRECTLY in Jesus' Passion seem
not aware of what I have just described. But that's
the way it usually happens. It is often after the fact that
we realize the significance of an event. This is particularly
true of our experiences of God. What happened to Moses
happens to us: We see only the Lord's "back" (Ex 33:23).

But what about the five friends who gathered at the
foot of the cross? It's really hard to tell from their silence whether they understood what was happening. Only
one person seemed to penetrate the mystery, and she apparently sensed something even before the plot began to
unfold. From a strict perspective, the text of the Scripture that describes this woman's role is not a part of the
Passion; in fact, Luke does not even write about it. For
this event took place "six days before the Passion" (Jn
12:1). But it forms a part of the announcements of Jesus'
death — a more concrete disclosure when compared with
Jesus' own verbal statements. This is why some Christian Churches open Holy Week with what happened at
Bethany, and this sign amazes us (Jn 12:1–11).

Imagine the setting: a banquet. One of the guests had
previously died. Only a few days or weeks earlier he was
buried in a tomb, and here he is eating just like everybody
else. Another guest, the guest of honor, starts talking about

---

*John 12:1–11.

18

his own impending death, even though he's not even sick: Jesus.

Then, during the dinner, a woman approaches Jesus and dares to waste a very expensive perfume by pouring it shamelessly on his feet. She lavishly dissipates a small fortune in a few short moments. If we believe the experts, the three hundred denarii that Judas complains about would represent an average year's salary today — thousands of dollars. To crown everything, Jesus, who is usually concerned about poor people, defends and even praises Mary's extravagance, of which he is the only direct beneficiary (though "the whole house was filled with the ointment's fragrance"; Jn 12:3). Anyone who does not understand and share Judas' protest, or the disciples' indignation in Mark and Matthew, either has already plumbed the mystery of Jesus or has only a superficial grasp of what was going on in this scene.

Judas could never have understood this woman's folly, he who sold Jesus out for a much cheaper price, the price of a slave, according to scholars. Many, on the other hand, understood something that concerns all of us — something that the Passion will reveal. An example will clarify this.

We love someone: For his or her birthday, for some holiday or anniversary we might spend money on a gift. We might try, if we have the means, to show our love by the amount we are willing to spend. In this way we attempt to express how precious he or she is to us. By the end of a lifetime the total of our expenditure might be impressive. Suppose we find out that this person we love is going to die soon. If we could, we would gather together all the gifts of our lifetime, all the money we had, *all our love*, and we would hand it to him or her all at once. Our extravagance, our waste would be an effort to show how much we love and how priceless our beloved is to us.

Mary understood that Jesus was precious, priceless. Already Sirach had said, "A faithful friend is beyond price, no sum can balance his worth" (Sir 6:15). But her wild behavior says more: "God's love, God as Love revealed in the human flesh of Jesus is priceless, beyond estimation and beyond imagination." I wonder if we put the same price tag on the priceless God — Love, on love itself?

Sarah, seven years old, says to her mother in front of me, "Mom, I know who your first love is." Yvette (who is a dedicated woman but with both feet on the ground) and I ask, "Who?" Answer, "Jesus." How many kids say that to their parents?

So God should be our most precious and priceless Love? Judas can help us here. In a very strange way, Judas speaks to us just as Mary did, but by his betrayal. As I said, Judas sold Jesus for a slave's price. He completed Mary's message and gave us a really surprising word, "slave." Jesus showed us a God beyond our comprehension: a Love who decided to take "the form of a slave," as Paul wrote, quoting an ancient Christian hymn (Phil 2:7). God *decided,* in Jesus, *to be our slave.* That is not our usual notion of God. The God of the Christian revelation is surprising.

It is good to remember that in the Jewish world of that time slaves did not find themselves in the infamous position that the word suggests today. However, slaves were the property of their masters and worked ceaselessly for those who possessed them (except on the Sabbath, if the master was observant). They were at the bottom of the ladder socially. A God who loves to the point of becoming a slave is really a priceless Love. Christians must believe that God decided to belong to us, to be ours. This Love who is from God and who dwells in us is handed over to us. In certain Christian Churches where the faithful receive the Bread that they believe is the Body of Christ, having God in the hand illustrates, in a very striking way, what I just said.

The Christian belief is that God works for us ceaselessly. God labors for us from our conception until our death, with no week-ends off or vacations, twenty-four hours — no, twenty-five hours a day, as a friend of mine

said. Unless we are blind, we can see this fact: As children we saw our parents working for us constantly, so God
in them. As adults, we only have to count the people who
make our clothes, produce our food, design our cars, pump
our oil, or generate our electricity from coal and atoms.
All over the world men and women are working for us
with the fruits of nature, already God's gifts. If we recall
that Love, *agape* in the New Testament, means first of
all to serve, then everyone and everything is the sign of
God-Love serving us.

It's surprising how much Mary and Judas reveal. Perhaps we feel an immense gratitude, like Mary, who really
understood Jesus. Do we want to imitate her, do what she
did, because of thankfulness? But Jesus is not in front of
us. What can we do to render love for love before a God
who serves us like this? There's a simple way: to serve
other people as much as we can, wherever we can work
for humanity. Working becomes anointing God, lavishly,
like Mary did for Jesus, by serving others as God serves us
in them. But Jesus himself suggests his favorite way, and
therefore God's favorite way.

Judas protests, "Why wasn't this ointment sold for three
hundred denarii, and the money given to the poor?" Thus
he makes a connection between Jesus and the poor. Jesus
goes back to it and asserts, "Let her alone.... The poor you
will always have with you, and whenever you wish you can
do good to them, but you will not always have me" (Mk
14:5–7; Jn 12:5, 8). Clearly enough, Jesus means, "Do the
same later for the poor." When we do our work well, it
is already excellent, but we are invited to serve the poor
lavishly, to waste our money and a lot more for them.
Our society certainly has a long way to go before being
reproached for such a waste.

There's a Christian organization in France whose members find a million ways to take care of the elderly poor.
One of their projects is to furnish each one with a free
vacation in a splendid villa, and at other times they buy di-

amond rings for golden anniversaries. One day an observer of their extravagances voiced his surprise at this waste to the founder of the organization, who answered him saying, "When we get to heaven, we will probably be surprised to see the kind of rags with which we have clothed Christ in his poor." They say that St. Lawrence the Deacon sold the Church's sacred vessels for the poor, and that some people were scandalized! When will we become Lawrences, inviting our society and our Churches to anoint the poor with a priceless perfume? The whole world would be filled with the fragrance of this oil, of this Love.

Money

THE PRECEDING CHAPTER suggests that we take the time to examine one of the principal players in the Passion drama: money. Money frames the account of Mark and Matthew. The latter begins with the money wasted by Mary in Bethany and ends with the payoff given to the soldiers for lying (26:7; 28:15). Mark starts in the same way but concludes with the women bringing the herbs they bought to embalm Jesus' body (14:5; 16:1). Money is mentioned in Luke too. It appears in John with Judas' reaction to Mary's costly gesture, and the apostle is described as a thief (12:3, 5–6). Money is there seventeen times in the four accounts — a significant fact. We frequently overlook this side of the Passion. Is money, in this context, making us uneasy? Could it be that we often pretend to know nothing about it while we place too much importance on it in our lives? Might this be because we are aware of allowing ourselves to be bought off too easily, or of having sold our soul, our convictions, the poor, without too many scruples? The Passion is a graphic example of all that.

This is the story of an innocent man condemned to die, even though he preached and lived the love of neighbor in a beautiful way. This is already an injustice. But on top of this we have money throughout the whole affair. However, the presence of money in the Passion says forcefully that when the Just One, when any just person, is condemned and assassinated, we can suspect that, for reasons more or less hidden, a price has been paid.

For Christians, God sent the Son to save us. Theologians in times past proposed the idea that God, in Jesus, paid a ransom to deliver us from captivity (1 Cor 6:20). This is an image that we can relate to because of any kidnapping, but one that raises questions. Would God have paid the Devil? But then the Devil would have had some power over God, as any creditor has over a debtor. The ransom notion has been put aside by most scholars.

We can penetrate the mystery of money in the Passion of the Just One by a simpler route. An old adage says, "Watch and see who profits by the crime." The unjust condemnation of an innocent person should always lead us to look for the interests that are safeguarded by the injustice.

In the Passion, Pilate and those who hold power in Israel seek, among other goals, to protect their jobs that included both power and money. The name "Mammon," in Matthew and Luke, personified money as a potentate: Money brings power and being in power brings money (Mt 6:24; Lk 16:13). Any organized and institutional group in human society always strives to preserve their power and their income. The problem *here*, in the Passion, is that the attachment of the Jewish leaders and the Roman procurator to their jobs leads them to sacrifice the One who had become a threat. "The worries of this world and the lure of riches choke the word" of Love in Jesus through the action of the ones in power (Mt 13:22). The Innocent One pays the price of their private interests that they understand and defend very well. Also, Jesus drove the merchants out of the Temple; the price of his boldness against the financial-political-religious institution had to be paid (Jn 2:13–16).

I stressed the word "here" above because what we see in the Passion has been a constant in human history. How many innocent persons have paid the price of the selfish interests of people who enjoyed power? The reasoning of

Caiaphas before the Sanhedrin has been repeated by many, "You don't seem to have grasped the situation at all; you fail to see that it is better for one man to die for the people, than for the whole nation to be destroyed" (Jn 11:49–50). "For reasons of State, for the good of the business, for the honor of the family, for the glory of the Church," have been stated reasons for which innocent people have paid the price, sometimes with their lives — reasons invoked to mask more sordid motives.

But I run into the same phenomenon at an individual level when I sacrifice some innocent person for my own protection or benefit. In order to achieve my career goals I neglect my family; to conserve my lifestyle I refuse to pay taxes or cheat on my tax statement and thereby diminish public aid to the poor; to increase my wealth I play the stock market but at some point in the game some people lose their jobs. This slaughter of the innocent lambs goes on at all levels of the social ladder. We are all Pilate and Caiaphas who succumb to the seductions of Mammon, and others pay the price. No question, "it is easier for a camel to pass through the eye of a needle than for one who is rich to enter the kingdom of God!" (Mt 19:24).

But the expression "to pay the price" evokes other scenarios. How many athletes, artists, and researchers have accepted to pay the price of a victory, a masterpiece, or a discovery? How many people have paid the price of fidelity without compromising their values or faith? The desire for physical or esthetic, scientific or ethical achievement has led legions of men and women to sacrifice many things, sometimes their lives. Examples abound of those, who, for the love of their neighbors or their country, for the love of the poor or of human rights, or for the love of God have paid the price.

In the Passion, God accepts to pay the price of a flawless love, of which we are the beneficiaries, even if we are Pilate or Caiaphas. "What proves that God loves us is that Christ died for us while we were still sinners," says Paul

(Rom 5:8). God-Love is extravagance. Jesus, in the Passion, lived out his own preaching, God's own word: "Repay to God what belongs to God" and "You can't serve God and money," he said (Mt 22:21; 6:24). In these words, he gave absolute priority to Love over whatever Mammon, thus revealing how God spends when it is a question of love. But he also invites a man "to sell everything he has and to give the money to the poor" (Mk 10:21).

There again he was announcing God's way of acting, for God gives us a fine example of this in Mary in Bethany, and in the women coming to the tomb. They all came to Jesus, spending their money to take care of him at the moment that he took his place among the poor ones of the world.

Sent by God, they were the living and human proof of God's care for his "Beloved Son," if we believe Christ's words, "No one comes to me unless sent by the Father" (Jn 6:44). Through those women, God shows us that money is not bad in itself (we cannot live without it, it is the price of our daily life). But by them, God tells us the inestimable value of money when it is used in the service of Love, and particularly the love of the poorest ones. When it is the price of Love, money, like everything else, becomes priceless — and most of all when it is spent on those who cannot pay it back (Lk 14:13–14). The money spent by the women for Jesus, God's Poor One, frames the Passion, as I said at the beginning of this chapter: It symbolizes the price that God accepts to pay in Christ for all of us, the whole human race. We cannot not make a return because we were too poor. In fact, we can, and the rest of the Passion will show us how, more and more clearly.

Robbed?

THERE ARE SOME CHARACTERS that we come across when reading the Passion who are so unremarkable that we forget them. We don't know their names or exactly who they were. However, what happens to them tells us something precious and, if the evangelists talk about them, it must be meaningful.

Before celebrating the Paschal meal, Jesus says to two disciples, "Go to this man in the city and tell him, 'The Master says, "My appointed time draws near. I am to celebrate the Passover with my disciples in your house"'" (Mt 26:17–19). Mark and Luke give more details:

> As you go into the city you will meet a man carrying a pitcher of water. Follow him into the house he enters and tell the owner of the house, "The Master has this to say to you, 'Where is the dining room in which I can eat the Passover with my disciples?'" The man will show you a large upper room furnished with couches. Make the preparations there. (Lk 22:7–13)

Mark states that the room is "all prepared" (Mk 14:15).

This is a strange story but not any stranger than another one that relates an event that occurred a few days earlier. Before entering triumphantly into Jerusalem, Jesus says to two disciples:

> Go off to the village facing you, and as soon as you enter it you will find a tethered colt that no one has

yet ridden. Untie it and bring it here. If anyone says
to you, "What are you doing?" say the Master needs
it and will send it back here directly. (Mt 21:1–9; Mk
11:2–3; Lk 19:28–40)

What a cavalier way in which to treat somebody else's
property! Let's overlook the mysterious aspect of Jesus describing an event before it happens; it is no doubt linked
to the text of the prophet Zechariah that foretells this happening (9:9). But what does that matter to the owners of
the ass's foal that Jesus is astride or to the proprietor of the
upper room where he will celebrate the washing of the feet
and his last supper?

Did these people know Jesus? Had they let him know
that they would be glad to help him out? At least it seems
clear that Jesus knew he could borrow the animal or the
room. But the brief texts don't bother to tell us about that
in the same way that they don't name names. This is an
invaluable anonymity because it lets us insert our own
names, for these two stories may not be as foreign as we
may think.

All parents have had the experience many times of
love demanding what belonged to them. The child who
looks for attention or affection, or even a friend who needs
this, comes to us and borrows or takes something of ours.
Whether it be our time, our smile, our money, or our listening, it is always our love. Often this happens without
warning, without a chance to prepare. The demand is there
and won't wait. Those who come with their request know
they can ask because we are always ready. Our "yes" is assumed in advance and required so urgently that we have
just enough time to acquiesce.

Love knocks at our door, "Look, I am standing at the
door, knocking. If one of you hears me calling and opens
the door, I will come in to share his meal, side by side
with him" (Rv 3:20). If we do answer and open the door
of our heart, Love enters as our Owner, exults, and serves.

Love celebrates a banquet that nourishes the person who knocked at the door of our heart. And sometimes the celebration is a surprise party like the welcome given to Jesus when he entered into Jerusalem, humbly and triumphantly victorious (Zec 9:9). We rejoice that something was asked of us and we give thanks, "Blessed be the one who comes in the name of the Lord!" (Mt 21:9; Mk 11:9; Lk 19:38, which adds, "He, the King").

An elderly man collapses on the sidewalk. People going by rush over; cars stop. Everybody takes care of the sick man. I go out of my way to inform the administrators of the convalescent home where he lives about what has just happened. I arrive at my meeting late but light-hearted.

In this best-case scenario our response to Love who comes and borrows all that we are and have is stamped with surprise. It is rapid, clear, and generous. We disappear behind our gift because, after all, it's the gesture that counts. Love fills the scene and we are dissolved in anonymity.

One evening our neighbors' little boy interrupted our supper and became the center of our dining room as he curled up on my wife's lap. Both of us melted with tenderness. After he left, our evening resumed, bathed in the grace of this disturbance. We were full of joy.

There are other things that happen to us that remind us of one of Jesus' parables where he talks about another anonymous homeowner. "You may be quite sure of this, that if the householder had known at what hour the burglar would come, he would not have let anyone break through the wall of his house." Admittedly, Jesus talks about the end of time, and invites his disciples to be ready, for "the Son of Man is coming at an hour you do not expect" (Lk 12:39–40). But isn't it also about the end of our peace and quiet when love arrives unexpectedly, piercing our walls and stealing our gift. We have all been "robbed" of our love by our children and our friends (not to mention the government that makes us work for the common good by exacting taxes!). At the beginning of the way of the cross, Simon the Cyrenian is "robbed" too (Mt 27:32). Oh, if we had known in advance what would happen to us, we would have done something to protect ourselves! As if we could ever protect ourselves from love! My little neighbors teach me this continually.

It is true that we often know how to guard against love. We put off visiting a friend who has financial problems so that we won't have to become lenders; we know we could not refuse to help, because of love. We pretend not to see or not to understand the behavior of a child because we don't want to be available and we can foresee our vulnerability. We take French leave at the end of a meeting so as not to be collared by someone looking for volunteers; we know we would say yes. Who has not run away for fear of being "robbed"? But who has not been "robbed" without later experiencing joy? And who has not been a robber?

The triumphant entrance of Jesus into Jerusalem and the preparation of the Passover meal are inseparable from the Passion narrative. The stories of the two anonymous householders that I just recalled are a transition to the drama of what Jesus is about to suffer for the salvation of all of us. Isn't it the Son of Man who intruded on the property of others so that Love could triumph there, and the One among us who broke into God's heart? After all, God had robbed him through the Canaanite woman, who stole the cure of her daughter, and especially through the woman with a hemorrhage who broke in on him and was cured (Mt 15:21–28; Mk 5:21–24). So before God he could be a thief in his turn. Many spiritual authors have called him the "Divine Thief." And he is that for us, when we are robbed or robbers, but so much more for God.

Indeed, the God revealed in Jesus' Passion is a love that asks for only one thing: to be robbed. Jacob's combat with the angel to wrest God's blessing attests to that (Gn 32:23–33). Jacob incurs an injury, but wins. Though Jesus still bears the stigmata in his glorified body, he won. Paul expresses this victory over God quite well: "Now that we have been justified by his blood, it is all the more certain that we shall be saved by him from the wrath" (Rom 5:9).

Nothing is more terrible than impenetrable people. It's true that they may look strong, but they never let themselves be robbed. Blessed be our God who is not like them. In fact Jesus said:

> Is there a man among you who would hand his son a stone when he asked for bread? Or would hand him a snake when he asked for a fish? If you then, who are evil, know how to give your children what is good, how much more will your Father in heaven give good things to those who ask him! (Mt 7:9–11)

Who is the God described by Jesus when he talked like that about prayer? The Almighty? Quite amazingly weak, in fact, faced with us, always children, always small . . . always ready to rob.

The Washing of the Feet*

J OHN OPENS his thirteenth chapter by striking a solemn note, as in the overture of an opera:

> Jesus knew that the hour had come for him to pass from this world to the Father. He had always loved those who were his in the world, but now he showed his love for them to the utmost. They were at supper, and the devil had already put it into the mind of Judas Iscariot, son of Simon, to betray him. Jesus, aware that the Father had handed everything over to him and that he had come from God and was going to God, rose from table.... (13:1–3)

Indeed, these are the opening lines of the whole Passion to come. But more immediately we are amazed by the apparently minor action that these majestic words introduce. Jesus washes his disciples' feet. I'm calling this a minor event because we find no trace of it in the other Gospels, not even in Mark who, according to the Scripture scholars, wrote under Peter's direction (Peter, one of the principal players in this scene!). If Matthew, Mark, and Luke say nothing about this occurrence, it must be because it was not particularly significant for them. It may have taken John years of meditation to fully comprehend the meaning of what Jesus did that night.

---

*Jn 13:1–15.

Yet the introduction seems to say that the whole Passion, the whole mission of Jesus might be exemplified in the washing of the feet. It suggests that if the Son had come into the world simply to accomplish this ordinary gesture, this would have been enough to reveal both Jesus and God. So it is understandable that for centuries some Churches have considered the washing of the feet one of the sacraments. In some congregations it is still a liturgical practice, and not only on Maundy, or Holy, Thursday.

For John this is a *sign* in the full sense of this word. Jesus descends to the lowest place, the place usually reserved for a slave. As I said, for the Jews, the notion of household slave was not encrusted with the pejorative and humiliating nuances that it has taken on today. Nonetheless, slaves belonged to their masters for the length of their slavery and were supposed to perform the most menial tasks, such as washing the dusty feet of whoever entered the house. A slave had no freedom, but Jesus chooses to take this position freely. He belongs to his disciples and serves them, *freely*.

Peter is shocked to see Jesus assuming the role of servant. After all, Jesus is the Teacher. According to the social protocol of that time, he is the one to be waited upon. What is this world coming to if the great ones start ministering to the poor? Would a CEO put himself at the service of the workers on the assembly line? This turns the world order upside down! Peter does not understand, as it happened the first time Jesus announced his Passion (Mt 16:21–23). So he refuses to be washed: "Lord, *you* wash my feet? No, you will never wash my feet."

Jesus chooses very strong words to respond to Peter's protest: "If I do not wash you, you will have no share with me." Aside from the pain Peter would have felt at the thought of having no share in Jesus' inheritance, John sees something else. We can understand Jesus' words in this way: "If you will not let me act as I wish, to be the one I want to be, you can't share in my heritage." And here is where we enter into the mystery that Matthew, Mark, Luke, and even John might not have immediately penetrated.

The first level of interpretation is linked to what will take place in the hours to follow, the Passion. In washing their feet, Jesus, as a slave, is in the lowliest human condition. He gives himself freely in total dedication and humble service to his disciples. This is a summary of the Passion. From this night until Friday afternoon Jesus will be on the lowest rung of the social ladder. He is an innocent victim in a religious trial the outcome of which was decided in advance. Secular justice will spare the life of a dangerous criminal rather than his. He will be condemned to death and executed among convicted criminals. He is handed over to his persecutors. And the scandal of the cross, which will be a problem for many of the first Christians, echos Peter's scandal when confronted with Jesus at his feet. Where now is the glorious Messiah expected by the disciples?

We know that these men used to discuss who would be the greatest among them, who would sit at the right hand of the Lord (Mk 9:33–34; 10:35–37). Their last question would even be, "Is now the time you are going to restore the royalty in Israel?" (Mt 9:33–34; 18:1–5; Mk 10:35–40; Acts 1:6). Hadn't Jesus himself said they would "sit on the twelve thrones to judge the twelve tribes of Israel?" (Mt 19:28). However, Jesus had been clear about this point. He had said:

> You know how the ones who are called the leaders of nations lord it over them and how great ones make their power felt. It can't be like that with you: anyone among you who wants to become great will be the servant of the others, and the one who wants to be first must be everybody's slave. (Mk 10:42; 9:35)

Since there is always quite a distance between words and actions, gestures are often more effective than fine phrases. So there he was, on his knees, at their feet, instantly extinguishing in them any political ambition that the triumphant parade into Jerusalem may have ignited a few days earlier. At the same time he kindles within them a flame that burns at another level.

For them, Jesus was speaking and acting in God's name, revealing in his own behavior something about God. Who has not associated God with power? We talk about the Almighty One or the Supreme Being. In the sense that this means that God has power over every creature, the notion has merit. But suddenly Jesus is showing his disciples *another* God. In his own way, while describing the washing of the feet, John repeats the ancient Christian hymn Paul quotes for the Philippians: "Though he was in the form of God, he did not deem equality with God something to be grasped at. Rather, he emptied himself and took the form of a slave" (Phil 2:6). Here, God is revealed in Jesus as the One whose power is invested in becoming ours, in becoming freely our slave. To my knowledge, we don't often hear God defined as our slave, as Someone spending time serving us, as the One at our feet in total freedom. A God like that is a wonder-ful surprise.

Picture the most tender mother washing the feet of her children, with the same care for each one of them. It does not matter if Simon the Zealot is tempted by violence and Judas by money, if Thomas is full of doubts and the sons of Zebedee are looking for the first seats, if Andrew is obliging and Peter brags . . . each one gets the same love. This is what God does for you and me, though we might be "poor, crippled, lame or blind" (Lk 14:13, 21).

That explains John's preamble, because what we see there is a phenomenal revelation. This is the kind of Love that God is — a Love capable of doing everything for us, a Love asking us to let that happen, and only desiring one thing: to belong to us and to serve us to the end. There are unfathomable depths in this statement. It is not only because we can't understand what it meant to be a slave in those days in Israel. It is because this expands our horizons in our journey toward knowledge of God and of Love, opening them into the infinite. In the face of the God revealed by Jesus Christ in the washing of the feet (and later in the Passion,) we can only "bend our knees" in our turn (Phil 2:9–11). For this "surpasses in length and width, in height and depth...our comprehension" (Eph 3:14, 18–19).

We might well wonder why we have pushed this definition of God aside instead of constantly returning to it in gratitude. Perhaps it's for the same reason that bothered Peter.

After having washed their feet, Jesus said to his disciples:

> Do you understand what I have done for you? You call
> me Master and Lord and what you say is true, because
> I am. If I who am Master and Lord have washed your
> feet, then you should wash each other's feet. Because
> I have given you example so that you too will do what
> I have done for you. (Jn 13:12–15)

"Do you understand?," he asks. We probably don't want to understand. Or maybe we understand *too* well the price to be paid for having a share of the inheritance of this God, this Love that Jesus reveals. Later on, Paul understood and he says as much when he writes to the Corinthians, "Even though I am not bound to anyone, I became the slave of all" (1 Cor 9:19).

It is not only a question of reversing a hierarchy of power to which we have grown attached. We must *freely* choose to become slaves of our brothers and sisters, men and women of our day. We are invited to use our freedom to belong to them and to put ourselves at their service (Gal 5:13). Doing this, we have our share in Jesus' heritage, in the inheritance of the God he reveals. We have a share in the life of unconditional Love that is God.

*Two guards in a prison in Connecticut were in charge
of issuing jail clothes to newly admitted inmates. Both
felt embarrassed because many of the jail pants had
buttons missing where there is normally a zipper. The
two guards volunteered to sew buttons for the inmates' pants. Their lieutenant taught them how to
thread a needle, as his mother had showed him.*

Somewhere within, we know the price of this love. It is
a Passion in the two ways of understanding this word that
I have explained. It requires a passionate love because it
leads to death. We lose our own life (Mt 10:39). Our in-
stinct for self-preservation and our permanent selfishness
rebel, are shocked, are bothered and refuse. No one likes
to die, but someone might be willing to die for love (Jn
15:13).

Paul, after having described Jesus humbling himself and
serving, shows how God exalted him (Phil 2:9–11). Where
can we see exaltation in the washing of the feet? It's simple. Is it not a glory for Love to love until that point? Before
Jesus, who washes the feet of the disciples (and later before
the Crucified One), we can't help crying out, "What Love!"
"You are my servant...through whom I show my glory,"
God had said (Is 49:3). Astonishment or surprise, admira-
tion or disbelief, I don't know which will come first for us
when we contemplate this scene. I only know that finally
we will be held in awe and gratitude and invited to plunge
into that ocean.

I will never forget an experience that gave me and some
of my friends a glimpse of this inheritance of Jesus. We
were volunteers giving retreats in prison where we would
always open the second evening, before celebrating the
Lord's supper, with the washing of the feet. Volunteers and
prisoners would wash one another's feet: Men, women,
ordained ministers and lay people, Native Americans and
whites, blacks and Latinos all joined together. We invari-
ably experienced something of "that One whose power in

us is capable of doing so much more than we can ask or imagine" (Eph 3:20). We knew each time the grace of becoming, like other people in other circumstances, some part of the mystery that was described so well by the German philosopher Hölderlin: "For God to be powerful is nothing. But to be nothing at all, that is really divine."

The Lord's Supper:
A Celebration of Liberation*

T HERE THEY ARE, the disciples gathered around the
One who in their eyes enjoys a special relationship
with God and, therefore, speaks and acts in the name of
the God of Israel. He probably presides over the Passover
meal.

This meal is invested with a particular significance because it commemorates the Exodus. Centuries earlier, the
Hebrews celebrated the Passover by standing while eating a
sacrificial lamb. The blood of the lamb marked their doors
and preserved them while the angel of God was inflicting a
last plague upon the Egyptians, the death of their firstborn
sons.

There began the liberation of the men and women who
would become, under Moses' leadership in the desert, the
nation of Israel. So Jesus' last supper with his disciples
is immersed in this context of liberation. In Egypt, the
Hebrews had been slaves in every dimension of human
life, politically, socially, and economically. Even their sex-
ual freedom was restricted, for the pharaoh had forbidden
them to have sons. During the Passover meal the Jews
would remember the liberation from these various forms
of slavery.

---

*Mt 26:26–30; Mk 14:22–26; Lk 22:14–20; 1 Cor 11:23–26.

The disciples had to have been poignantly aware of
this context of liberation when they celebrated a Passover
meal. Israel, subjugated by Rome, was not a free country.
Periodically the Jewish people had risen in revolt against
the pagan occupation of their land. There was in fact a
strongly revolutionary faction, the Zealots, who militated
for the political liberation of their country. Maybe the disciples thought, "Which blood of which lamb will save us
today?" (Ex 12:1–14). Remember their last question to
Jesus, "Is now the time that you will restore the royalty
in Israel?" (Acts 1:6). In a surprising way for his friends
dreaming about freedom, what Jesus does that night is
connected with the liberation of the Exodus. He will be the
true Messiah of a real freedom.

This tells us, already, that our eucharistic celebration
omits something vital if it is not connected in some way to
the liberation of the people of our time, ourselves included,
at every level of human life. The Lord's supper cannot be
for Christians merely a pious encounter with Jesus, either
individually or among friends. It must also be the place
where we are nourished for acting on behalf of the liberation of all those who suffer oppression of no matter what
kind, because oppression is sinful. The historical context
of Jesus' last supper is enough to establish this as necessary. In one sense, the urgency that moves Jesus to eat
this last Passover has to do with this: the right of Israel to
be free. Jesus of Nazareth, in Galilee (site of frequent rebellions against the Roman pagans) could not have been
untouched by the absence of freedom suffered by his people. He is too well acquainted with the compassionate God
of the Exodus listening to the Hebrews' cry of complaint
(Ex 3:7).

We will never know what was going on in the hearts of
the disciples present at this meal. However, a simple reading of what went on there, a reading based on a common
structure of our life can give us a lot to think about.

He takes bread and wine and gives it to them saying,

"Take this, and eat it, take it and drink it. This is my body, this is my blood." Christianity abounds with theological explanations of these words. Did those present have any trouble accepting them? I don't think so. They had had many opportunities to witness the efficacy of Jesus' word. He had healed the sick and cast out demons, multiplied loaves and fishes, calmed the storm and brought Lazarus back to life. I like one particular example: One day he said to a paralyzed man, "Your sins are forgiven." And faced with a negative reaction by some observers, he added, "What is easier to say, 'Your sins are forgiven,' or 'Get up and walk'?" And he healed the man. It seems to me that this was his rationale: You doubt my effectiveness in what is unseen; so, I will do something very visible to convince you (Lk 5:17–26).

So the phrase "This is my body, this is my blood" must have been regarded by the disciples as an efficacious word, even if they had not yet had the opportunity to elaborate a theological explanation. We, in our day, can still follow Jesus' reasoning. Which is easier, to change bread and wine into something else, or to transform the heart of this man or that woman who finally turns toward God or to the service of others? Maybe our questions about the Eucharist are signs that we can't see the other miracles around us every day — miracles in the hearts of individuals touched by the efficacious word of God that turns their lives around and "makes all things new," new bodies (Is 43:19).

Jesus says, "Take," offering this bread and wine. If I hand you my Bible and say, "Take it," you understand that I am giving you a *gift*. Since "Body and Blood" is a Semitic expression that means, "Everything I am, my whole life," the disciples understand that Jesus is giving them the gift of himself. But if I give you my *own* Bible, you will surely perceive that my gift is, at the same time, a free *sacrifice*. Gift and sacrifice are inviolably bound together in Jesus' gesture. If I give you my Bible, I must certainly consider you my friend. But if I give you my life, it is more than friendship — it's love, as when people who are in love say to each other, in words and actions, "Take, here is my body." Jesus, by giving himself, as bread and wine, showed his *love*. In the form of food, Jesus accomplished his own words, "There is no greater love than to give your life for the ones you love" (Jn 15:13). That cannot escape the disciples because it is in the structure of an ordinary event of our life: each time we give or receive a gift.

The disciples have at the same time an individual and a collective experience. I, Peter, I, Matthew, I, John, I take and eat this food that "is" Him — if I take these words literally. But then he unites me to him. I know that Jesus has at his disposal God's forgiveness — as the story of the paralyzed man reminds us. So in this union that he brings about, all distance from God disappears — from the God whose forgiveness he is. There is a reconciliation between me and God that takes place by this act of Jesus. When two persons are united, we often use the word "covenant." Between God and me, Pierre, me, Matthew, or me, John, Jesus establishes or reestablishes the covenant. The term is used in all the texts of the New Testament that include the Passover meal of Jesus. But there is another side of this experience. I, James, I, Thomas, I see the other disciples having the same experience as I have. A common experience binds us together. To listen to the same orchestra, to eat a meal together, unites us. When we welcome a mutual friend at the airport, he or she unites us. It was the same thing that night. The disciples have the experience that Jesus' gesture was uniting them in a *common union*, a communion. They became one through him.

So what is happening is a covenant in several ways. A personal covenant between each disciple and God, a covenant made with one another, and a covenant between the whole group and God in Jesus' action. The uniting power of every meal that we have together reaches a peak here. It is as if the life, the love of Jesus filtered down into the body of the disciples right to their fingertips — the way all food does.

We need to go back to a point noted earlier: For the disciples, Jesus speaks and acts in God's name. For the ones who are there, God says something through this communion. I interpret this Word of God like this:

I love each and every one of you. Through Jesus, I love to the point of giving you my whole life. All my life because he is my dearest one, my beloved on whom my favor rests. All my life, too, because he is alive with the same life I live, Love. Recall what he said, "The Spirit of God is upon me...He has sent me to bring good news to the poor, to proclaim liberty to captives, to restore sight to the blind, and announce on behalf of the Lord, a year of grace." Now this life is yours, in your whole being. (Lk 4:18–21)

Here is where we find the liberation that Jesus carried to the depths of its effectiveness, to the level of his new commandment, "Love one another as I have loved you" (Jn 15:12). By this movement of common-union he destroys all antagonism and separation. He builds bridges: He is the Bridge (Pontifex in old Latin hymns) between each one of us and God, between all of us and God, between all of us. The disciples could not then be other than bridge-builders.

Breaking bread in his remembrance makes them ice-breakers, peacemakers. "Blessed are the peacemakers, they shall be called sons (and daughters) of God," he had said (Mt 5:9). Yes, they become this. And they will establish communities where liberation will exist at every level, because in the Church there was no longer "male or female, master or slave, Jew or Greek" (Acts 2:44–45; 4:31–34; Gal 3:28; Phlm) Indeed, there is still much liberation to be done, but the Church ought to be the witness and the leaven in this world of all true freedom. Starting with its own. Paul admonishes a community who is celebrating the breaking of the bread while in the midst of division. In the measure that the Corinthians would do nothing to heal their separations, they would be eating their "own condemnation" (1 Cor 11:29). The same is true for us. It's not for nothing that from early times the Christians have repeated, "The Church makes the Eucharist. The Eucharist makes the Church." The word of Jesus on the bread and on the wine framed the Paschal meal, for he is the Alpha and the Omega of our liberation, of our communion.

So the God who Jesus reveals in the Paschal meal is a God who desires to liberate all human beings so that they can live as brothers and sisters in peace. This is what the God of Exodus did for the tribes of Israel. But the action of Jesus in the Eucharist implies even more — a Word about God. If the action of God accomplished in Jesus Christ frees us and unites us in a life of love, making with us a community, isn't it because the One Christians call God is for them a Trinity of Persons perfectly equal and free, a perfect Community of Love?

Bread given, wine poured out: In community, another God is revealed.

The Lord's Supper: **Eucharistein**

WHEN I GIVE YOU my Bible, as a friend sacrificing what belongs to me, what will be your first reaction? Probably you'll say, "Thank you."

I can't imagine any other response than that in the disciples' heart, even if it took other forms. In fact, could they have acted differently from their Teacher? Before giving them bread and wine Jesus gave thanks. This is reported by Matthew, Mark, Luke, and Paul.

It is very good to stay for a while with this unfathomable mystery. The One whom God calls "Beloved Son" gives thanks. Usually, we pass over these words rapidly. Yet they are able to create in us a space as infinite and as intimate as the one existing between God and God. For the first time in history, in Jesus, a human heart and human lips give perfect thanks to God. Surely, John faithfully recorded for us all that he remembered about the discourse following the Passover meal. And he remembers a lot! But still it is very little. The other evangelists don't breathe a word about it. I like to view all the words of John and the silence of the three synoptics as a proof of the impossibility of expressing the depth of this prayer of Jesus.

We can only imagine: Jesus being grateful for Mary and Joseph, for his first teachers of the faith, for all his companions, male and female, including the ones present there that evening, for the crowds and the sick. And our faith will enable us to realize that this thanksgiving covers all humanity and the cosmos, from the Alpha to the Omega. *For everyone and everything.* I would love to end here and say, "Period." But it is not a period that should end our contemplation of Jesus giving thanks. Musicians would indicate a pause, in order to permit us to sense the thankful dialogue that continues eternally between the Persons in God. God thanking God.

We have all known moments in our life when we have brushed up against something like this at a deep level. We may have, for example, experienced an intense communion or reconciliation within ourselves or with others, and then our gratitude and our thanksgiving was so immense that words failed us. One of the best examples I can give of this from my own life occurred recently. I had asked my friend and neighbor, six-year-old Paul-John, to help me fill the birdfeeders because I had a broken wrist. After working with me, my little friend heard me saying, "Thank you." He replied, "Pierre, thank you too. For you let me help you." Which one of us was more grateful? Probably God.

To the extent that the disciples grasp the gift they receive, they say, "Thank you," in their own way. The Greek Churches said *eucharistein* — from which we get the word "Eucharist." First and foremost the celebration of the breaking of the bread and the gift of wine is to say, "Thank you." We have thousands of reasons to thank God. For our health, for time, for peace, for friendship (1 Cor 4:7). But above all we need to thank God for the inestimable gift of Jesus and for all the gifts received through him. We need to thank him particularly for the revelation of a surprising God.

Remember that for the disciples Jesus speaks and acts in God's name. In his last meal he reveals a God handed over to them, as gift and food. In one sense this is not new for his friends who are Jews like him. They know that God was connected with life. They have learned through the Old Testament, the book of Joshua for instance, that the final proof of God's merciful and lifegiving action toward Israel is the fact that they are eating the fruits of "vines and olive trees" that they have not planted (Jos 24). That night, once again, they receive the same sign, a food they have not cultivated.

Jesus had often nourished them by his love and through his word over three years. But this time he becomes himself visible and palpable food, this bread and this wine in their bodies. The God revealed by Jesus in his banquet was not a God who is God knows where, but a person materially present and handed over to them, shared by them — a God they can taste, handed over down to this last crumb, this last drop. These last words are not simply an image. John sees this gift again in the last drops of blood falling from the side of the Crucified on Golgotha (Jn 19:34).

The fact that God nourishes us like this calls into question the word, the nourishment, and the community we are for each other, and together for the world. Using the image of a meal, we must examine ourselves on the kind of food we give to our communities and our contemporaries, we Christians, we the Churches of Christ. If we are the cooks, we are called to be *chefs* and not *hash slingers* — and above all when we serve the poor.

Surely, we can give them food. But we are invited to do more than that, to give ourselves. God begs us to do this as Jesus does when he invites us to do this in remembrance of him. Gratitude pushes us to enter into the spirit of the same love with which we are loved. The disciples were already following Jesus and wanted to be with him. Their dedication to their Master later became an offering of themselves to him, "Take [Lord], this is my body. Take, this is my blood." That is not surprising because the spirit of love is reciprocity. As I said, two authentic lovers say *to each other*, "Take, this is my body." If we are conscious of the gift that is given to us, gratitude flows into our heart. And in our turn, we want to hand ourselves over to God, making our own the words of Jesus about the

bread and wine. But what does it mean to hand oneself
over to God?

If we look at how bread finally arrives on our table, we
discover that all of humanity is behind it. The farmers cultivated the wheat and harvested the grapes, the bakers and
the wine growers made the bread and pressed the wine,
the truckers transported it all. The workers manufactured
the trucks and the chemists developed a better gas, the ge-
ologists and cartographers located the oil fields. In short,
through Jesus, the gift of God as bread and wine comes to
us through all of humanity. If we follow the Spirit of God's
act of love, we can make some return to God by giving
ourselves to all the humanity that surrounds us. Through
Jesus, we hand ourselves over to God saying, in word and
deed to the people around us, "Take, this is my body.
Take, this is my blood." And we become for others "true
food [and] true drink" (Jn 6:55). Significantly the Christian
communities celebrate the breaking of the bread using the
words used by Jesus himself. Around the table we say to
the whole world, often through the one celebrating in our
name, "Take, eat, this is *my* body. Take, drink, this is *my*
blood." We make Christ's words our own words.

If we take Jesus' words and ourselves seriously, in making his words our own, the consequence is clear: We certainly nourish one another, and together we nourish men
and women around us with the gift of our whole lives. We
make of ourselves, through the power of Jesus' word, food
for all the hunger, drink for all the thirst of our contemporaries. This might have been in Paul's mind when he
wrote to the Corinthians celebrating the Eucharist, "You
announce the death of the Lord until he comes" (1 Cor
11:26). Yes, we must be the new body of Christ handed
over to the world until the end of time. And if we do this,
we can expect to see the evidence. I mean that the world
around us would give thanks for the Church, its presence
and its action, just as we give thanks for what Christ did
and does for us. If the world withholds its thanks, per-

haps something of Jesus' meal got lost along the way in his Church.

Therefore, when we give ourselves to others in our life, as a spouse and parent, or as a friend and neighbor, or as a worker and a citizen, we celebrate a eucharist — *the ordinary eucharist of our daily life*. And when we celebrate as a community the Lord's supper through the ritual of our denomination, *we celebrate liturgically what we live daily*. The eucharistic celebration and a daily life of service are the two sides of the same coin.

We celebrate the exchange of love between God and us through Jesus. Everything in our daily activities becomes grace. God-Love is given to us in everything and everyone. We give ourselves in return to God, through others.

We can give thanks to God, and certainly God thanks us gratefully.

The Lord's Supper:
Two Copper Coins*

W E CAN LOOK at Luke 21:1–4 as a supplement to our meditation on the Lord's supper. The evangelist recounts the story of the widow who let slip into the Temple almsbox two copper coins — the smallest change of the money of that time. Jesus notices her donation and says, "She, from her want, has given what she could not afford — every penny she had to live on." He praises her more than all the rich donors who give "out of their surplus."

When we celebrate the Lord's supper, we may feel that the thanks we tender and the gift we make of ourselves are nothing when compared with what Jesus offers, what God gives. This is certainly true. But if we are waiting to make a gift equivalent to God's, we will wait a long time. The widow's story can liberate our hearts and allow us to offer ourselves without shame.

This woman brought all of her poverty, her want, the little she had to live on. Two copper coins. But this little was put into that big collection box at the entrance to the Temple that was called "God's Treasury." As soon as the gift was put into the Treasury, it was engulfed in the mass of money that was accumulated there. And, I might say, it assumed the proportions of the Treasury of God itself.

*Luke 21:1–4.

There is another scene in John's Gospel that has the same meaning. Jesus, in John 6, is concerned about feeding the crowd that follows him. He tells Philip to do something about it. The disciple finds only one boy with five barley loaves and a couple of dried fish. "What good is that for so many?" Andrew worries (6:9). There are around five thousand people! But when the loaves and the little fish are put into Jesus' hands, they are multiplied and nourish the whole assembly. Even the abundance is such that there are twelve baskets of leftovers.

We really don't have much to bring our God, just our indigence: two little coins, a little thank-you, and a little gift. But let us slip ourselves into the thank-you and the gift of Christ himself in the eucharistic prayer. Then our gratitude and our gift will take on the proportions of the thanksgiving and the self-donation of Christ, for the salvation of the world, for the immense joy of God.

This is exactly what happens each time we celebrate the Eucharist. We bring our bread and our wine to God, poor bread and poor wine of poor people, incapable of becoming divine by themselves. But all of that is made divine by Jesus' word and action. However, without those coins, without the loaves and the fish, without the bread and the wine, nothing would happen. No money for the Temple, no food for the crowd, no Body and Blood of Christ. This seems to be the way God has decided to proceed.

We are indeed poor, but our surprising God dares to need our poverty to enrich all humankind (2 Cor 8:9).

The Agony*

A T THE END of the evening spent with his disciples Jesus goes toward what some might call his fate. But it is not a fate, a destiny, because he knows where he is going and why he is going there. It is a choice, as it is obvious in John's account where Jesus appears as the master of the events — as the Son of God. "Get up! Let us leave this place!" (Jn 14:31). He leaves the warm and secure circle of his friends and goes out to face the storm that is about to be unleashed upon him. He risks everything.

We remember Peter when he risked getting out of his boat to go forward on the tumultuous waters of the Lake of Gennesaret (Mt 14:22–33). And he walked on the waves without any trouble so long as he kept his eyes on Jesus. But as soon as he took his eyes off his Teacher and looked at the wind, he sank. The same thing is true when we face storms in our life. We won't sink so long as we focus on the deepest reasons, love for instance, that motivated us to accept the risks we have taken. And so throughout the Passion, Jesus does not waver or sink, most probably because he continued to keep his heart and his will anchored to his deepest desire. "From John the Baptizer's time until now the kingdom of God has suffered violence, and the violent take it by force," he said (Mt 11:12). For the sake of God's reign, he goes into the storm. He knows the verse, "I keep

---

*Mt 26:36–46; Mk 14:32–42; Lk 22:40–46.

the Lord before me always, for with God at my right hand,
nothing can shake me" (Ps 16:8).

However, he does lose footing for a short while, and
this makes him more approachable when we are hesitat-
ing before the radical consequences of our decisions. He
vacillates in the garden of Gethsemane, where his agony
starts the cycle of violence into which he is going to be
plunged. Although I won't insist upon the physical aspect,
because the Gospels don't, violence is everywhere in the
Passion. There is the noise that reverberates throughout
the texts and that is striking against the contrast of Jesus'
silence in Matthew, Mark, and Luke. We hear a cascade of
words, shouts, and mockery. We have also all that pushing and shoving from every direction, which we have seen
when I spoke of Jesus being handed over. Jesus was treated
as many prisoners have been. Finally, we witness all the
rough handling and wounds inflicted on the Innocent One.
The whole ensemble is like a tidal wave that seems to en-
gulf him. But the Passion also implies another violence, an
interior kind, climaxing in his agony.

The agony implies a contrast that we often overlook. If
Judas finds Jesus easily that night, it is highly likely that
they all used to spend time there regularly. This peace-
ful place had probably been the scene of restful gatherings
among friends. Now it becomes the ground of a terrible
solitary interior battle, made worse by the very presence of
sleeping friends. The same contrast exists in a wake when
people are socializing and even laughing, not too far from
the family who is weeping. For Christians, the agony is the
equivalent of the riverford of Jabbok where Jacob wrestled
all by himself with God's angel and came away blessed but
forever wounded (Gn 32:23-33).

Who can say, beyond the stylized evangelical phrases,
what went on between Jesus and God during those hours?
It might be better to use Scripture to interpret Scripture
in this instance. The Servant Songs in Isaiah, for example, Jeremiah 11:18-20, Psalm 22, and other psalms of

lamentation, or even Sirach 51 may help us to imagine the
dialogue. Who knows what goes on in each of us when
we go through this kind of agony? In some pages of *The
Strength to Love*,* Martin Luther King, Jr. tells us what
he went through one night in his kitchen. He took a hard
look at whether or not to go ahead with his project to op-
pose racism. He knew that it might cost him his life. At
dawn, after a night spent agonizing, he made his decision:
He would continue to fight for Human Rights, and this
commitment led him to his assassination.

This is only one example. Perhaps we ourselves have
known this agony in more ordinary circumstances, when
we had to choose between the risks required by our love for
someone or something and the temptation to preserve our
security. The decision to speak frankly to someone close
to us about things that are certain not to please is made
in agony because the friendship is at stake. To blow the
whistle on someone for the sake of social justice and at
the risk of losing one's job is made with personal suffering. To demonstrate public opposition to a government, a
union, or a Church implies dangers that render this decision painful. A person has to withstand violence in order
to stay his or her course in the face of the storm, in the
face of fear. When Jesus spoke about the kingdom taken
by violence, he predicted that he would undergo violence
himself, though he was the Son (Heb 5:7–10).

This kind of wrenching of the heart can go further.
Sometimes we have to make decisions that may threaten
our own life and what we cherish the most, as well as
the lives of others. Resisters to dictatorship in many countries have faced the fear of their own torture and death,
the fear about the fate of their families, the fear that they
might, under duress, betray their deepest convictions. It is
at this level of descent that we get an idea about Jesus'
agony. Only those who have never experienced this agony

---

*New York: Harper & Row, 1963, chap. 13.

can regard the bloody sweat described by Luke as a roman-
tic notion and in bad taste (22:44). Since Jesus was human
like us, he must have been shaken by the fear of suffering
and death. Loving his disciples, he must have been concerned about what might happen to them because of him.
(Didn't he say to those who arrested him, "If I am the one
you are after, let these others leave"? — Jn 18:8.) Wish-
ing to reveal God's love to people, he certainly knew that
to waver would destroy the credibility of his message; God
would not be revealed as he desired. Here something important must be said, which we often forget because it did
not happen.

Suppose Jesus had given in to violence and wavered.
History abounds with examples of people who have wavered at the moment of trial. And only those of us who
have never given up at the final moment may have the
right to cast stones (Jn 8:7). Some have not been able
to endure under torture and have finally abjured, or even
have joined forces with the enemy. Others have re-emerged
later, absolved by society and often without being judged
by those who underwent the same atrocities without falter-
ing. It is so human not to be a superman or superwoman!
In the days of St. Augustine, the Church learned how to
embrace once again Christians who had apostatized during
the years of persecution. The Church did this, many times,
at the request of the very ones who had not denied their
faith under torture. Through this struggle, the Church discovered that it could forgive anything. So could we have
forgiven Jesus if he had faltered? Maybe. But this weakness
would have hurt our faith in the God to whom he gave witness. Would God have been the "one to speak and not act,
to decree and not fulfill" (Nm 23:19)?

How could we believe in a God as loving as we hope for,
ready to die for us in spite of everything? Paul would never
have been able to say, "The proof that God loves us is
that Christ, while we were still sinners, died for us" (Rom
5:8). The Love that is God would not even be as big and

free as the love we have seen in men like Gandhi, Martin
Luther King, Jr., and Archbishop Oscar Romero, in women
like María Elena Moyano (symbol of nonviolence, killed in
Peru, 1992) or Aung San Suu Kyi, Nobel Peace Prize win-
ner in 1991 (imprisoned in Burma because of her struggle
against dictatorship), just to mention a few, but also in less
famous men and women who have given their lives for
love.

Caught in storms, a multitude of martyrs kept their
liberty intact and stood firm in their convictions. Do we
think that God, in Jesus, could not?

> If God is for us who can be against us? Who will sepa-
> rate us from the love of Christ? Trial, anguish, perse-
> cution, hunger, nakedness, danger, the sword? ... Yes,
> I have the assurance that neither death nor life, angels
> nor principalities, present nor future, nor powers, nei-
> ther height nor depth nor any other creature will be
> able to separate us from the love of God that comes to
> us in Christ Jesus, our Lord. (Rom 8:31–39)

It is because of the grace of Jesus' agony that we can, as
Christians, share Paul's certainty when we face violence.

Worse than all of that, a compromise between Jesus and
his adversaries would have damaged a very profound bond
of love. Dealing and settling would have meant the disso-
lution of an incomparably intimate union. Here we come
to the core of Jesus' agony.

Backing off would have meant accepting that violence could separate him from God. Violence can separate
human beings. In the agony of Jesus humanity tried to
use violence, like a wedge, *to separate God from God* —
if we believe that Jesus is the Son of the One he calls
"Abba, Daddy." Our words cannot describe the heart-
rending depth of Jesus' agony. Paul uses an expression so
strong he wrote it only once, "The One who never knew
sin was made sin by God for us" (2 Cor 5:21). God the
all Holy is linked for all eternity to the One we call the

Son, and repelled by Sin: The apostle tries in his metaphor to express how much God and God are at the same time united and separated. God, one and torn apart.

That is nearly impossible to penetrate. However, many parents have experienced agony like this when their child intruded himself or herself between them and thus tried to break their bond, more or less deliberately, by an act of violence. Many couples have felt such a wedge driven into their mutual love by in-laws. The agony of Jesus has been shared by many men and women, but his agony struck God directly in the heart. At the core of Deity, as Meister Eckhart would say.

The example of parents allows us to grasp something of Jesus' victory. A mother and father, who stand fast in their mutual love and in their love for their child, finally overcome the violence done to them. Through suffering they grant to the torturer what is most necessary and life-giving, their indestructible and unconditional love. So human violence is crushed in the strong embrace of the will to love of the Persons of the Trinity, Father and Son united by the same Spirit. Thus, violence in its attempts at separation is forever thwarted and we, humankind, obtain henceforth what we most need: the proof that God's love for us is *absolutely* indestructible, and therefore really unconditional, no matter what we do against it.

God is not a love like ours that often bargains, setting conditions, "I will love you if you behave, if you are polite, if you do what I want, if you give me this; God, I love you if..." God says to us through Jesus in the Passion, "I love you. Period," meaning "with no ifs, ands or buts." When God is Love with an "if," it's this way: "I love you, even *if* you don't love me."

Could God have intervened in order to change the course of events? After all, Jesus says in Mark, "Father, you have the power to do all things" (14:36). In Matthew he says to a disciple during the arrest, "Do you not suppose I can call on my Father to provide at a moment's notice

more than twelve legions of angels?" (26:53). If this had
happened, we would never have known in such a dramatic
way how much God loves us. In this agonized "yes" of
Jesus, in the "Yes, let's go" of his Father who does not in-
tervene, we hear for the first time and forever God telling
us *all* about divine love. The rest of the Passion will just
unfold what is already there in its totality in the Garden of
Olives.

Sometimes our love is too weak and fails the test. But
when we tested God through the actors of the Passion,
God-Love did not flinch. The Passion of parents to which
I have alluded is one facet of the Passion of the Persons of
the Trinity for each other — and together for us. This includes both senses of the word "Passion" described earlier.
Peter sank because he stopped looking at Jesus. Parents
who keep the love they want to live before them, men and
women who never stop contemplating the ultimate purpose of their life, Jesus faithful to his Abba... all tell us
how to avoid sinking and how to proclaim the fantastic
strength of love in the face of violence.

If the agony happened at that level, then it is no wonder
that Peter, James, and John were incapable of being present
to Jesus. How could they enter into God's agony? Jesus
cried out, "My soul is sorrowful to the point of death" (Mt
26:38). Yes, it was in the Garden of Olives that Jesus began
to die, and on this path no one can go with us. Similarly,
it's very hard for us to be present to two people whose
love for each other is torn apart. We are torn as well between the desire to stay and the urge to leave. If we stay
with them we feel heavy and inadequate. We don't know
what to say (Mk 14:40). And here is where we hear the
most human and pathetic cry of God ever uttered through
Jesus' lips: "Stay here and watch with me" (Mt 26:38). God
has never needed us and our presence so much as at that
moment, even if our presence is impotent. Love never so
much needs our presence, apparently powerless, as when
our brothers and our sisters are in agony. We can always

be there like the angel in Luke's text; we can comfort *even when we can do nothing.*

We will see later that there are many situations and places in our society where love is in agony. We can always provide our presence. In fact, it is at these moments and in these places — in our gardens of olives — where our love is tested. If we, Christians, love to hold vigils in our churches on the night between the Thursday and the Friday of Holy Week, let's hope we also keep as constant a watch with human beings in agony.

Nonviolence

T HERE IS ALSO in the Passion the usual violence we see between individuals or groups. All those in league against Jesus — priests and scribes, elders and their assistants, Herod and the mob — are involved in active violence. Surprisingly, Jesus' usual enemies, the Pharisees, are barely apparent in Mark and Luke. John briefly mentions them as the ones who sent their agents to arrest Jesus (18:3). In Matthew, they only show up after Jesus' death in order to assure that the tomb will be well guarded (27:62).

The Gospel writers never explain this strange disappearance. Could it be that those Pharisees wanted to preserve their purity in what would transpire? This would fit their thinking and behavior. Or were they like all the people of history who have worked behind the scenes to assassinate the reputation, the career and the life of innocent people — only to eclipse themselves at the moment of the actual kill? Or could they have been worried primarily by Jesus' religious teaching and threatened by the prospect of his confirmation through his resurrection? This might explain their intervention in Matthew. Or did the issue of the Pharisees receive special treatment by the evangelists because Joseph of Arimathea, Nicodemus, and probably some other Pharisees had become Jesus' disciples? Scripture scholars still debate these questions, but one thing is certain: The Pharisees practiced the Law and defended it, but they had no authority to enact it. This responsibility

belonged to the priests in terms of cult; to the scribes in
terms of interpretation; to the elders on the social level.
These men had the power. The violence of the Passion
points out clearly who has the power.

This is particularly evident in the pagans' violence. Pilate, in the first place. He has Jesus scourged even though
he is innocent. Symbol of the power of Rome, he has the
final say in pronouncing the death sentence. The soldiers,
extensions of his power, enjoy torturing one more Jew in
Jesus. We can apply to the authorities acting against God's
anointed one, Jesus, what Psalm 2 says, "Why do the nations rage and the peoples utter folly? The kings of the
earth rise up, and the princes conspire together against the
Lord and against his anointed."

Between the Romans and the Jews hangs Judas, as the
catalyst for violence. He is on the Romans' side because he
paves the way for the death sentence, but he is not one of
them. He is on the side of the Jewish leaders because he
actualizes their plot and hands Jesus over to them, but he
is one of the Twelve. Like any traitor, he is no longer a part
of the group he betrays, and will never belong to the group
he joins. Judas is from nowhere in the Passion. Being neither Jew, nor pagan, nor disciple, he no longer has a home.
"He went out" of the intimate community gathered around
Jesus, and finally he withdraws entirely from the human
circle by his suicide (Jn 13:30; Mt 27:5). Where did he
go? The Church has never declared him damned. It would
be better for us to do likewise. We must leave it to God
to know to what extent the traitor is guilty. When people cut all bonds, the situation becomes God's business,
and God's only. We must just remember that whenever we
become a Judas we lose any possible home.

Another aspect of violence is the collusion of those who
do nothing to help Jesus, starting with his own disciples.
Peter seems to be the only one tempted by a violent reaction during the arrest. But we know how long Peter's
passionate protest will last. Also Jesus forbids him to be

one of those "who use the sword" (Mt 26:52). In the end, like the others, he too disappears and lets the enemies of his master and friend settle his fate. And what could he have done, anyway, against all the powers in league against the Christ? Did he think of Psalm 2, which said, "The kings of the earth rise up, and the princes conspire together against the Lord and against his anointed?"

We do see a disciple present in the courtyard who knew the high priest. Traditionally the Church has identified him as John, the same John who was also at the foot of the cross. But it looks as though he did not do too much to save his Teacher either (Jn 18:15). Isn't he like all those who look the other way when an innocent person is the victim of a violent act, those who absent themselves and let violence do what it will? Silence gives consent. We all have been cowards at one time or another, overcome by fear or impotent with shock and grief. It would be unwise for us to blame the disciples. First, we would have to be sure of our own courage and fidelity, to be certain that we have "no sin" before casting "the first stone" (Jn 8:7).

There were some people who seem not to get caught up in the wave of violence sweeping through the Passion. Unlike the others, they provide a compassionate presence. The women. Mary is the first one to demonstrate this kind of behavior by lavishly using her perfume. Then Pilate's wife intercedes for Jesus. Along the way to Golgotha we find the mourners — maybe they are only fulfilling their ritual task, but at least they weep. Present at the final moment are Mary, Jesus' mother; his mother's sister; Mary, the wife of Clopas; and Mary of Magdala (Mt 27:19; Lk 23:27; Jn 19:25). These women are there, silently risking the taunts of passersby. Is this an old cliché, repetition of the stereotype of the faithful and compassionate woman? Or is it an echo of Jesus' behavior, giving room and respect to women in a society where their voices usually went unheard (women would also be the first witnesses of the resurrection)? Indeed, in many cultures women have been closely associated with the cycle of life and death. But anyway we have here a lesson from the so-called weaker sex. The women of the Passion teach us how to be present to all those who are the victims of any kind of violence.

Often one particular instance of violence in the Passion is forgotten. Jesus' violence. One day a lawyer said to me,

> Jesus in his Passion makes me think of those Algerian resisters whom I had to defend in the French court during the Algerian war of independence from France. Fully aware of the risk they were taking, they assumed an attitude that was, in a way, violent both toward me and toward the judges. They refused openly to renounce their convictions.

In the same way, Jesus is the one who confronts his adversaries with their oppression. He puts them on the defensive. I will return to this point later.

John insists that Jesus is acting as the Son of God and therefore is the One who calls the shots. His Gospel shows Jesus discussing with Pilate, without fear. With a tone of authority unheard of in a defendant, Jesus reminds Pilate about the source of all authority. For Jesus, it comes from somewhere other than this world. For Pilate, it comes from the Emperor (18:33–37; 19:10–11). As far as the Jewish leaders, they appear to be on the defensive in all four Gospels, and this since well before the Passion (Mt 26; 21; Mk 14; 11; Lk 20; etc.). I don't dwell on Herod, oozing with sarcasm, who does not even merit a word from Jesus (Lk 13:32; 23:8–9).

We know that the way Jesus behaved toward the merchants in the Temple was an exception. John seems to excuse or justify this violence that was out of character for his Teacher on the grounds that "zeal for God's house" was the motive (2:17). If we want to find real violence in Jesus, we have to examine his consistent opposition to the power of oppression. Some people might bring up Matthew 23, a chapter apparently full of violent invectives hurled at the scribes and the Pharisees. The problem here is that we can't hear the tone of voice. I hear these words spoken in a loud voice, for sure, but fundamentally in a sad voice. I hear it as a last resort, a last attempt of Jesus' mercy. We have all spoken like this to people we love when we saw them going down the road to perdition. To read Matthew 23 in any other way is, in my opinion, a projection of our own violence onto Jesus.

God had already said, "Those for the plague, to the plague; those for the sword, to the sword" (Jer 15:2). "All who draw the sword will die by the sword," said Jesus (Mt 26:52). He refused any kind of physical violence in his life, in the same way he refused to be made a king or a political messiah. He did not accept James' and John's suggestion that he call down fire and brimstone on the inhospitable Samaritans. Just as he abstained from using the sword and from asking his Father for twelve legions of angels when he was arrested (Jn 6:15; Mt 16:20; 17:9; 26:52–53; Lk 9:54–55).

Jesus' way of acting was similar to those since his time who have promoted nonviolence, for instance, Gandhi and Martin Luther King, Jr. He never expresses hatred or threats aimed at his adversaries. He does not force them to lose face. He treats them so calmly or so silently that he reveals their violence, a violence he refuses to cooperate with. At the most he sends them back to their own words. Finally, we find no trace in Jesus of any kind of vengeance. "I gave my back to those who beat me, my cheeks to those who plucked my beard. My face I did not shield from buffets and spitting," said the suffering Servant in Isaiah (Mt 26:63–64; Jn 18:22–23, 37; Is 50:6).

This is the God of Jesus Christ: the One "who hates the lover of violence," the One who said to the beloved David, "You may not build a house in my honor, because you have shed too much blood upon the earth in my sight" (Ps 11:5; 1 Chr 22:8). God, the *Nonviolent One*. This is the way that God behaves with us. God has an unbelievable respect for all creatures and for human beings who have freedom and are capable of love. Love can never be forced, and God knows that. Jesus' behavior in his Passion destroys all images of God as violent because "God is Love" (1 Jn 4:8). A God who is "meek and humble of heart," who is like the Servant, "gentle and humble of heart... who will not contend or cry out... who will not crush the bruised reed, and will not quench the smoldering wick" (Mt 11:29; 12:19-20; Is 42:1-4). "Blessed are the meek," said Jesus (Mt 5:4). Such a beatitude fits him as well as the God of whom he is the witness. But gentleness does not mean weakness. Like the sap that opens the rose with a soft but astounding power, the meekness of Jesus is strong.

That is why we have to change our vocabulary. Jesus is not violent; he is *strong*. His strength unmasks the real weakness hidden behind the physical violence of his enemies. Physical violence is a language, often a nonverbal confession, the last resort of weakness. When we slap a child that's what we admit, that we have lost control of the situation and of ourselves. The slap proves that we have lost the capacity to convince by reason, and that we can only brutally silence the child and all that the child provokes in us and around us. We have lost the strength of gentleness. My example may be trite, but the same principle applies when a government fires on a crowd rather than listening and entering into a dialogue, and when a torturer executes his silent victim and silences within himself any compassion.

We all have the capacity for violence, and often our love is not strong enough to subdue it. We sometimes even mistake our violence for strength. We all need, individually and collectively, the gentle but strong power to love of the God of Jesus Christ in order to act less frequently out of weakness and violence. We need to ask for it unceasingly from the God of Jesus, who said through the prophet Hosea, "I will not destroy Ephraim again; for I am God and not man" (11:9).

The Arrest*

WITH THE ARREST OF JESUS we take the first in a long series of steps toward his death. The text suggests a certain deployment of forces. Jesus must have seemed really dangerous to the Sanhedrin. We are struck by the tragic absurdity of these great powers puffing up their ranks in order to crush innocence. But we know that Jesus' adversaries don't want to miss their mark, so they mustered all their strength in secrecy (Mt 26:4–5).

Are the disciples frightening the high priests and the elders? When John tells the story he focuses on Jesus, and so he does not say too much about the behavior of the apostles. But he criticizes the violence that Peter tries to start. How could these disciples have frightened anyone? Mark and Matthew don't show them any mercy at all. If we want a sentence that crystallizes their attitude at this crucial moment, aside from Peter's vague impulse to resist, it's this one: "They all abandoned him and fled" (Mt 26:36; Mk 14:50). The arrest, for the disciples, is the moment of desertion (Ps 38:12).

Do we remember all the times we abandoned our friends when the going got tough? Just as soon as trouble comes, and especially when authority speaks, we go away leaving those people on their own. This already shows us how strong our attachment is. But what if the one we desert is innocent? Have you ever noticed how people step

---

*Mt 26:47–56; Mk 14:43–52; Lk 22:47–53; Jn 18:2–11.

aside or sneak off when a witness to an accident is needed? It would do us good to remember, when that particular temptation occurs in our lives, what we felt when *we* were abandoned and most of all when we were deserted by the ones we really counted on as our friends.

I know a couple who were supported by many people at the wake and funeral of their child; months later, a deep depression engulfed them, but nobody called or wrote, no one came. A friend of ours lost her job, and she was having financial problems; we remember talking with her with gentle words, but did we pull out our checkbook? How about when someone in our office, right in front of us, begins to verbally harass a woman or mock someone who is handicapped? If there were an investigation would we claim blindness and deafness? We used to be very close to our neighbor but now, what can you expect, he is in prison! And as a nation, how many countries and peoples have we deserted? Just look around: Children are starving or hungry for nourishing food and where are we? "All we like sheep have gone astray; we have turned everyone to his own way" (Is 53:6).

We fled because we shrink before the call of compassion (*cum-patire* in Latin, "to suffer with"). We shrink and we are stripped naked. We appear as we really are. "He, leaving his cloth behind ran away, naked," says Mark (14:52). Nobody knows who this young man was who fled naked from the olive grove. Mark himself, since he's the only one who mentions it? Maybe Mark kept this man anonymous so that we could identify with him. And we can (2 Cor 5:10). Yes, when we abandon people to their miserable fate and above all when, though innocent, they are persecuted, our hearts are laid bare. Mark does not explain this evasion. This gives us a chance to look into the reasons for our own escapes. Why do we flee? The naked truth is that we are cowards addicted to comfort or to our careers, heros in words but not in deeds, rash fools who put ourselves needlessly in situations we can't handle. It is up to each of us to discern the motives for our own abandonments.

In difficult moments, the Tempter tells us, "Don't stay. Don't let love push you too far. You won't get out alive." Yet every Sunday we are there in church listening to sermons about love. "Every day I was beside you... teaching in the Temple," says Jesus in Mark and Luke. The closeness of Jesus, the Word of Love in the temple of our church or of our heart, doesn't bear much fruit in the hour of trial. The Tempter insisted, "It's too dangerous. Don't try to love till the end." And so we run away.

But even when that happens, Love says, "I am," (*Ego eimi* in the Greek text). John puts this expression in Jesus' mouth, probably remembering the revelation of God's name to Moses, "I am" (Ex 3:14). One meaning of that name is, "There I am, always the same." So John asserts that in Jesus Love is already near us, unconditional and indestructible, full of the compassion expressed by God in Exodus 3. There forever.

There when we are abandoned by someone. "When you pass through waters, I will be with you... When you walk through fire, you shall not be burned... Fear not, for *I am* with you... You are precious in my eyes and I love you," God said through Isaiah (43:1–5). We have within us enough strength and vital energy to pass through many ordeals. After all, those who have survived the hells they have gone through have shown a love for themselves that allowed them to survive the "power of Darkness" (Lk 22:53). And we can always give thanks for those who have been faithful to us in time of trial. They have been, they are the living proof that even if we flee, God never does. If we have not yet experienced abandonment, let us remember when the time does come the words of Isaiah 43:1–5, and Jesus during his arrest saying, "I am."

Still more astounding is the fact that Love is still there forever even if we should abandon somebody. Perhaps we have forgotten, ignored, or repressed our love in some terrible situation. We still need to believe in that presence that is never totally extinguished within us, that never fails completely. The possible word of love "is nearby [us,] already on [our] lips, already in [our] heart" (Rom 10:8; 5:15–19). If we abandon love, our power to love never abandons us. We can go back to it and to the one we have abandoned as soon as possible. "Come back to me with all your heart," says a song inspired by Hosea 2, which takes up a refrain so often heard in the Bible. "Return, return, O maid of Shulam, return, return," sings the chorus to Israel in the Canticle of Canticles, as do many scriptural texts calling the Jews back to their God over and over again (Sg 7:1). This permanent coming back is the whole history of God's People, and our whole story as well. But coming back to the Love that dwells in us is possible only if we believe that at the moment of our most wretched desertions, Love still says, "I am."

Not only does love remain within us even when we fail, but God respects what we can and cannot do — even to the point of letting us run away. Jesus interceded with his enemies to let his disciples leave: "Let them go" (Jn 18:8). He intercedes so that we can go away if we want to, if we can't do anything else. But Love stays there. A man was visiting his mother in the hospital. It was hard for him to cope with what he saw. She was in pain and had tubes attached to every part of her body. Seeing his distress, his mother whispered to him, "It's okay, honey. This is too much for you. Go." He fled. Her love did not change. This is what God does.

But can't we try to change our behavior? The arrest of Jesus calls out to us in many ways. Jesus does not hold the failure of his disciples against them. And we? Do we hold on to our anger and bitterness toward those who have deserted us? Can we forgive them? After all, we only perpetuate the pain of abandonment we have known if we refuse to forgive what they have done. If we have ever abandoned someone, the remembrance of this may help us to forgive. If that has not yet happened to us, it still may.

On the other hand, Jesus calls us not to forsake others. There are no crowds of visitors pressing at the doors of nursing homes, psychiatric hospitals, or prisons. Are we among those who abandon the elderly, the mentally ill, and prisoners? Of course, no one is asking us to be presumptuous and foolhardy and then cave in under the slightest burden; the Evil One knows how to play with a devotion that has never been examined through discernment. "It's not those who say, 'Lord, Lord' who will enter into the kingdom of Heaven, but those who do the will of my Father," Jesus warned (Mt 7:21).

So it is up to us to come back more often and with wisdom to this Spirit of Jesus who is within us, with all the power of the Love that is God. After assessing our own resources, like the wise man or the thoughtful king in Luke, let us try as far as possible not to run away, not to be deserters (Lk 14:28–31). Like the son who refused at first to do what his father wanted, we might have a change of heart and come back to our work in the vineyard, to love (Mt 21:29). If we believe that "God is faithful and will not let [us] be tried beyond [our] strength," more often than we think we will see that we are capable of being there and of saying, "Here, I am" (1 Cor 10:13).

The Trials: Judges on Trial*

I F I WERE ONE of the participants in a trial, I would not really enjoy the Scriptures that narrate the religious and civil proceedings that Jesus underwent before the Sanhedrin and before Pilate. In fact, we have all taken part in human trials as judge, prosecutor, defense attorney, witness, in one way or another.

So here we have Jesus faced with the religious and civil authorities of his day and their justice. He is condemned to death by both of them, apparently for different reasons. The Sanhedrin finds him a blasphemer according to the Jewish Law, but the Roman occupation forbids them to execute their sentence (Jn 18:31; 19:4–6.) Pilate sends him to be crucified as a rebel according to the Roman law. But the distinction between the religious proceedings and the civil trial is not as clear as it might seem.

For Jews and Romans the law of civil life was of religious origins. Read Leviticus to see that that applied to Israel. For the Romans who still believed that the Emperor, the origin of law, was divine, it amounted to the same thing. The first Christian martyrs in Rome died as insurgents and as atheists, for they refused to worship the Emperor. And if Rome let the Jews practice their faith at all, it's because the Jews were unyieldingly religious.

---

*Mt 26:57–67; 27:1–31; Mk 14:53–65; 15:1–20; Lk 22:66–23:25; Jn 18:28–19:16.

But other less noble factors lead to the condemnation of Jesus. There is a mixture of religious reasons or pretexts and political motives. Could this be why John totally ignores the trial before the Sanhedrin and mingles both the religious and the political aspects before Pilate? The Sanhedrin raises the most fundamental question with Jesus: "Tell us . . . whether you are the Messiah, the Son of God?" (Mt 26:63; Mk 15:69; Lk 22:70). But the evangelists also assign other motivations for the coming condemnation.

Jesus is arrested at night in an isolated area and not by day in a public place. The Jewish authorities act in this way "for fear of a riot among the people" (Mt 26:4, 55; Mk 14:2, 49; Lk 22:53). This is reminiscent of many police actions in countries run by dictators where the powers prefer the shadows "because their deeds [are] wicked." "Everyone who practices evil hates the light . . . for fear his deeds will be exposed," says John (Jn 3:19–21). To act out of fear like this "without creating a disturbance" does not resonate with religious motivations (Lk 22:1, 5). Was Jesus too popular for the Sanhedrin? The word "jealousy" in Matthew and Mark offers an explanation that points in that direction (Mt 27:18; Mk 15:10).

What kind of jealousy? The kind we know too well. The jealousy we felt as a child toward a brother or a sister more gifted than us or who got more attention. The jealousy that exists between the candidates in an election. The jealousy toward a colleague who gets a promotion before we do. The fear of losing our position as a beloved child, a sought-after office, or the esteem of our associates is the sting of jealousy — and we launch an attack.

We may tell lies about our competitor or publish his or her weaknesses. We defame our opponent and usually not to his or her face; we strike from behind, from the shadows. And what a pleasure to find false witnesses (Mt 22:59; Mk 15:59)! Talleyrand, one of Napoleon's ministers, used to say, "Calomniez, calomniez, il en restera toujours quelque chose!" — "Go ahead and drag him through the dirt; some of it will stick!" As members of our own local "sanhedrins," this is one lesson we have learned and practiced well.

Jesus' trial often surprises us with things we can't understand. Caiaphas says to us, "You have no understanding whatever! Can you not see that it is better for you to have one man die for the people than to have the whole nation destroyed?" (Jn 11:49–50). Excellent political reasoning for the survival of Israel (and a parody of Jesus' own words about cutting off the limb that leads us to sin) (Mt 18:8–9). No doubt the high priest is thinking of the good of the Sanhedrin as well, since the words "for you," translated sometimes "for your advantage," are sufficiently clear (Is 56:11). Yes, we might have an excellent political reason, but at what cost! "Straining out gnats and swallowing camels," priests and scribes keep themselves pure by not entering the praetorium, but their hands are already stained with blood (Mt 23:24; Jn 18:28). If we are shocked, maybe it is because we don't want to understand what concerns us.

In every society people have paid the price for similar reasons. A lot of immigrants, poor people, Jews (in Nazi Germany), communists have become the victims of this same kind of reasoning. But even in our own family or in our childhood games, haven't we persecuted and destroyed somebody for so-called good reasons? Reasons of State, of all kinds, have always hidden more base motives. Even the Church has not been exempt in its excommunications. Enmities can appear to have a religious basis where, in fact, they are founded on an egoism that exalts reputation, money, power or other inglorious considerations. For example, the lasting religious wars that followed the Reformation were fought not only in defense of dogma or the Scriptures.

In a strange way the men of the Sanhedrin express the truth of their deeds when they tell Pilate, "We have no king but Caesar!" (Jn 19:15). A true confession...because

they are more concerned about their own political interests than they are about what happens to divine Law. And
knowing that the Procurator is of the same mind, they can
easily get to him by saying, "If you free this man you are
no 'Friend of Caesar.' Anyone who makes himself a king
becomes Caesar's rival" (Jn 19:12). And Pilate, though
convinced of the innocence of Jesus, condemns him (Lk
23:4, 14, 20; Jn 18:38; 19:4, 6, 12). According to the evangelists, he knows what lies behind the behavior of the
Jewish authorities — jealousy. But "Truth? What does that
mean?" (Mt 27:18; Mk 15:10; Jn 18:38). He is not stupid!
He is not going to risk a riot that might ruin his reputation in Rome and cause him to lose his title of "Friend
of Caesar," if in fact he has it. And what they're telling
him about Jesus is that "He agitates the people," and "He
keeps people from paying tribute to Caesar." What civil servant would not be wary of this (Lk 23:5, 2)? After all, these
Jews have already shown what troublemakers they can be,
especially when they come from Galilee (Acts 5:37).

On top of that, what business of his are Israel's religious fights? Why should he jeopardize his peace and quiet,
his job, by rendering a just verdict that might foment a
riot in order to save some Jewish preacher (Mt 27:24)?
To make matters worse, the title "King of the Jews" is in
the air, even if it is really hard to tell in the heat of the
moment who gave this title to Jesus. But "Anyone who
declares himself a king is Caesar's enemy!" (Jn 19:2; Mt
27:11; Mk 15:2, 12; Lk 23:2; Jn 18:33; 19:14–15, 19–22).
This title will be used in mockery by the army rabble at the
praetorium and by the scribes and the priests at the foot
of the cross, but it must have been used first by Pilate to
condemn Jesus (Mt 27:29; Mk 15:18, 32).

We are all so happy when we find a "reason" to
justify our dishonorable decisions. "The poor drain the
public funds," we say to avoid paying taxes financing social programs. "Maybe these people are harboring spies,"
expressed the rationale for the abusive internment of

so many Japanese Americans after Pearl Harbor. "Those homosexuals are cursed," was the thinking implied by some preachers to justify their lack of compassion at the beginning of the AIDS epidemic. "Let's reveal to the public everything that happened so that such a crime will never be repeated" is the excuse used by the criminals, victims, and the media as well in order to make money by exploiting tragedy. Every family finds its leper for far from good reasons.

We are often Pilate. We started on this course by saying, "It's his/her fault," about our brother or sister as we lined up our excuses to avoid parental blame. Sometimes we are not smart enough to pile *all* sin on the scapegoat. It is expedient enough if we make even *one* big one stick; our victim is driven into the desert...where death awaits the scapegoat (Lv 16).

When he is faced with this parody of justice, Jesus turns his judges into defendants by his silence. *His trial is actually the trial of his judges* (Is 3:14). By his silence he refuses to be an accomplice to a huge farce; he refuses to feed the fire as we sometimes do with ill-chosen words. And when he does speak, he sends them back to their own words and deeds. "If I said anything wrong produce the evidence, but if I spoke the truth why hit me?" he says to the one who slaps him (Jn 18:23). "It is you who say I am"; "Are you saying this on your own, or have others been telling you about me?" he replies to the members of the Sanhedrin or to Pilate (Mt 26:64; 27:11; Mk 15:2; Lk 22:70; 23:3; Jn 18:34). His words send his adversaries back to their own plot and Pilate back to his cowardice. Jesus, in turn, gets silence: They evade him by taking another direction or by pushing on toward his condemnation, a sentence that has already been decided. What could they say in their own defense? Nothing. They are all guilty and they know it. And we know it too.

Since the covenant, there was one truth for the Jews: God is the real King in Israel. In Jesus, who always

preached the heart of the Law, this King is derided and
denied in the name of some other "kings" I have described. Jesus' trial repeats the case made by the prophets
against Israel and its idols. Even the pagan Pilate reminds
them of this truth by deciding to keep the inscription that
proclaims, universally, in the three languages spoken in
Palestine at the time, the royalty of Jesus (Jn 19:19–22).
On Golgotha Jesus' proclamation of the coming of God's
kingdom in Israel and its refusal of God's reign come to a
culmination. Through Pilate, the Gentiles refuse as well.
He who knows very well that behind the Emperor is Divinity sacrifices the God promised to the nations through
Abraham by handing over this King of the Jews as feed for
their idols. And all the others, the pagan soldiers and the
Jewish crowd, join in the derision. Paul might have had all
of that in his mind when he wrote Romans 1–3 about the
universality of sin and ended with, "There is no just man,
not even one" (Rom 3:10). But we, what do we do?

"May your kingdom come," we pray. Yes, in these words
we say that God-Love is our King, but how do we treat
this King? We often push Love behind the other kings of
our hearts, our idols that are the same ones that Pilate
and the men of the Sanhedrin served. We laugh at Love
when we believe it is incapable of the miracles that can
be accomplished by money or power, fraud or dishonesty,
lies or violence. We all prefer our Barabbas to Jesus (Mk
15:7, 11). "Perform a miracle; then we'll believe in you,"
we snigger before people who are trying to love, at great
cost, in their family, in society, or in their Church (Mt
27:42; Mk 15:32). It sometimes takes the voices of nonbe-
lievers to remind us that the truth of human relationships
lies in respect and love. It wasn't the religious institutions
that wrote the Universal Charter of the Human Rights; the
United Nations did that.

In fact, whenever in our thoughts, judgments, or actions we condemn Love, we are the ones who are judged.
"It is you who say I am": Jesus' words invite us to check

out if we think and act according to our faith in him, who is supposedly our King. A king is first. Is our King, Love, first in our life (Jn 18:34; Mt 27:11)? At least we could pray for the grace of rescuing Love: "Lord save the king!" "Let the king live on and on.... Assign [our] Love and Faithfulness to guard him!" (Ps 20:9; 61:6–7).

But the silence of Jesus refuses to condemn anyone who has failed. And when he says, "Father, forgive them. They do not know what they are doing," the silence of the Father answers. The silence of the Father who gives consent.

The Trials: The Law on Trial?

FOR MANY FIRST CHRISTIANS, who were ex-Jews, the condemnation of Jesus by the keepers of the Divine Law was a stumbling block. Paul, the former Pharisee, is the most striking example of this fact. It would take him years to find an answer, written in Galatians and Romans. These ex-Jews had always sung, "The Law of the Lord is perfect, refreshing the soul" (Ps 19:8). And Psalm 119 had always been dear to their hearts.

Yes, Jesus seems to disobey the Mosaic Law. He touches a leper or a dead body; forgives people or decrees that sins be forgiven; eats with sinners; takes liberties with the rules that govern food, ablutions, and the Sabbath day; forbids divorce and does not condemn the impure woman who touches him (Mt 8:3; 9:11; 12:2, 10; 15:2, 10; 19:6; Mk 5:34, 41; Lk 5:21; 7:14; 13:14; 14:3; 16:18; 19:7). But these are only *a few* examples out of all of his public life.

So this suggests that Jesus *usually* followed the Law. I'll come back to the times when his behavior was the exception to the rule. However, he asserts that he has come "not to abolish the Law but to accomplish it." This is clear when he asks his disciples to do better than the scribes and the Pharisees. Exegetes say that he constantly sends the Jews back to the very heart of the Law: "Love your God, and your neighbor as yourself" (Mt 5–7; 22:34–40; Mk 12:28–31; Lk 10:25–28).

Did Jesus want to update the observance of the Law? This is always necessary with any law. The Law was considered to be divine since it was inspired by God to Moses. But it had been expressed, written down, and interpreted by people of a particular place and historical situation. Jesus knew, for example, that the two texts of the Commandments differed. One version based the Sabbath obligation on the Creation event; the other on the Exodus. One includes a man's spouse among his possessions; the other does not (Ex 20; Dt 5). In the same way, when we want to update the meaning of the expression "We, the People," we include in it blacks and Native Americans; in 1776, they were not included. Concerning interpretations, we only have to change a few Justices and many things are no longer constitutional in the United States. Will the laws of 1994 still be appropriate for 2094?

But, like today, in those days specialists implemented the precepts of the Law. Jurisprudence was a part of their task, which resulted in an accumulation of writings. Leviticus is a good example of that. But how does the value of these additions compare with the core of the Law? That's what Jesus was asking when he accused the Pharisees and scribes saying, "You put aside the commandment of God to observe human traditions. . . . In this way you nullify God's word for the sake of your tradition which you have handed down" (Mk 7:8–13; Mt 15:1–6; 23:16–23). Jesus, like a good lawyer, but without any degrees, sends the purists of his time back to the heart of the Law in order to renew the understanding and practice of it. Is that why he was condemned?

Others have been condemned for this: the first feminists asking for the right to vote for women; the first Native Americans demanding the restitution of their land; the first prisoners complaining against inhuman conditions of life in prison; the first union members who fought for just wages. These are some examples. In the tragedy of Sophocles, Antigone, in the name of an unwritten law, rebels against her uncle King Creon and the laws of her city that forbade her to give her brother a decent burial.

This is not only a Greek tragedy of centuries ago, for the same thing happens every time someone demands a law that is more up-to-date, and is condemned for it. Those who hang on to the letter of the law are at least hanging onto the past, and maybe to their own privileged status. History never proves them right because time does not flow backwards. But their actions have preserved for the future the essentials of what was written yesterday. Jesus was doing that when he centered everything on the heart of the Law. So why condemn him?

I said he had no academic degrees. Nonetheless, his authority stunned the crowds and irritated his adversaries (Mt 7:29; 21:23-27; Mk 1:22, 27; 11:28-33; Lk 4:32-36; 20:2-8). Was he an authority because he was inspired by the essence of the two commandments? For instance, he cures a woman on the Sabbath. When the head of the synagogue reacts to this Jesus cries out, "O you hypocrites! Which of you does not let his ox or ass out of the stall on the sabbath to water it?" (Lk 13:15). What could his enemies say? They could not blame him who was caring for his neighbor, while they were caring for themselves through their own animals. They knew the commandment he often quoted, "Love your neighbor *as yourself*" (Lk 14:1-6; Mt 12:9-14).

But his authority came from another law, so *other* than the Mosaic Law that Paul invents the expression, "the Law of Christ," and he summarizes it, as Jesus did: "The whole Law has found its fulfillment in this one saying — You shall love your neighbor as yourself" (Gal 6:2; 1 Cor 9:21; Gal 5:14). *The Law of Love.* What makes the Law of Christ something new? The written law was for the good of the tribe and could not foresee the individual case; this is inherent to any written law. Love, on the other hand, in Christ's Law, seeks the good of each individual in his or her particularity. That's why the too-literal application of a law to an individual can create harm, as the old Latin saying asserted, "Summum jus, summa injuria" ("The rigor of the law creates extreme injury.") Here is an example of the inadequacy of the letter of the law when it is pushed to the extreme.

In 1992, the Supreme Court of the United States admitted as not unconstitutional the kidnapping, in another country, of a criminal wanted by U.S. justice. The explanation offered by the Justices (the majority) was that nowhere in international agreements about extradition was kidnapping literally forbidden. The minority opinion, as well as the opinion of other countries, was opposed because that judgment obviously went against the purpose and the spirit of the treaties governing extradition: to respect national sovereignty.

On the other hand:

A car is racing through traffic in a big city. The driver runs all red lights, slaloms around other vehicles, and blows his horn incessantly. When the car finally screeches to a halt in front of a building, the two police officers who are chasing the car stop too. The driver jumps out of the car and yells to them, "Hurry! Let's bring her to the emergency room! She is about to deliver her baby!" (The driver was my mother's obstetrician).

Love has its own law. "Love has never known any law," sings Carmen. "The heart has reasons that reason does not know," said Pascal. So when Jesus has to choose between the letter of the Law and his love for a particular person, his answer to the situation creates an unavoidable conflict with the Law. The story of the adulterous woman might be the best example of such a conflict (Jn 8:1–11). The woman is guilty, according to the Law, and she must be stoned (Lv 20:10). The Pharisees and the scribes are *in*-side the Law, she is an *out*-law. Jesus neither approves the Law nor condemns it. Beyond these extremes, he is *elsewhere.* As Love, and this is literally true in the text, he is *with* the individual who needs mercy and compassion while his adversaries are with-out. He just invites the woman, "Don't sin anymore." But he does not judge or condemn *because this is not the work of love.* This is the way we should understand Jesus' exceptional behaviors: Usually his love follows the Law for the good of the group, but when it is unavoidable to choose between the Law and Love, Jesus chooses Love. As Love, he could not help to appear as the master of all law, including Mosaic Law.

There is the real reason of his condemnation. It is difficult to know if Jesus said he was the Son of God in the sense that expression would have for us today, but he certainly acted like he was. He called himself the Son of Man. That refers to Daniel 7, where a "Son of Man" receives from God "dominion, glory, and kingship" on all "nations and peoples of every language" forever. He shows a similar sovereignty in his mastery of the Law when he forgives or declares that someone is forgiven. And his adversaries are not mistaken when they say, "Who is this man who utters blasphemies? Who can forgive sins *but God alone?*" (Mt 9:1–8; Mk 2:1–12; Lk 4:21). So Jesus claims by his words and deeds to enjoy a unique intimacy with God. This is blasphemy for his enemies. This justifies the last sentence about Jesus and the Law that we find in John, which condemns him to death, "We have our Law, and according to that Law he must die because he made himself God's Son" (Jn 19:7).

The scandal of the Jewish leaders is heightened by a surprising reality for them. When God gave the Law to Moses, it was as the Almighty with thunder and lightning, smoke and fire on Mount Sinai (Ex 19). If only God had appeared in Jesus with the power of Isaiah's vision, or the splendor of Solomon's Temple, or as a Messiah crushing Rome "with an iron rod... [shattering it] like an earthen dish!" (Is 6; Ps 2:9). His adversaries reveal something in their mockery on Golgotha: "Let the Messiah, the King of Israel come down from that cross here and now so that we can see it and believe in him!" They are expressing their expectation and therefore their error (Mk 15:32). For them the Law was much less connected with justice than with power. Their scandal is understandable, for they have before them an ordinary carpenter! If God is really in this powerless man from Nazareth, God must be really a *small* God. A God they don't know! "You know neither me nor my Father," he told them one day (Jn 8:19). To be more precise, they knew, but did not recognize this God.

For Jesus shows them their God: God, in Jesus, became *small for those who are small, anaw for the anawim.* The Jews should have recognized this God from their history. This is the God who chose Israel, a *small* nation, instead of Egypt or Babylonia. Today God might have chosen Monaco over China or the United States. With the same logic this God became present in the man from the small hole in the wall that was Nazareth — "Can anything good come from Nazareth?" Nathanael had asked (Jn 1:46). The same principle pushed Jesus toward the lost sheep, the outcast, the sinner. This is the God of Israel choosing "worm Jacob...maggot Israel" (Is 41:14). This was the heart of their Law because it was the heart of their God who had always begged them to care for the *anawim*, the powerless and voiceless, who was now begging them to have mercy on this *anaw* from Nazareth, Jesus.

Jesus did not put the Law on trial. "The law is holy, the commandment is holy and just and good," said Paul. But "sin found its opportunity and used the commandment: first to deceive me, then to kill me" (Rom 7:11–12). Jesus' trial is the trial of those who make and apply the law. The preceding chapter showed that the masters of the law could use it for their own interest. Here, their sin is not to see the challenge of their God "Blind? If you were, you would not be guilty, but since you say, 'We see,' your guilt remains," says Jesus to his adversaries who blinded themselves (Jn 9:41).

As Love, he always invited them to open their laws, ears, and eyes to what life says and shows them, like the differences made by history in the two texts of the Ten Commandments. Life is not with the past, the elders, and the status quo. As one translation of Qohelet says, "I observe that all who *live* and move under the sun side with the child, the second and the usurper" (Eccl 4:15). Jesus, when he faces the experts of the Law, is not the God of our Mount Sinai, justifying our desire for unjust power. He is, for us, this love who usurps the power of our laws, so that they become justice, unceasingly renewed like a family by a new child — justice of the present moment and, above all, justice for the small ones, the *anawim* of today.

The Trials: Victims on Trial?

S OMETIMES THE PASSION makes us angry with the innumerable victims in history, especially those who are poor and powerless. First, we become angry about the law itself. The law was not written by and for the carpenter of Nazareth, exactly as it can't be written today by the poor, because the poor don't write law. The law for the poor, which may or not be valid, is written by people who never were or are no longer the voiceless poor. Jesus was condemned by a law written by the educated men of his time who held power. The white law that governs the blacks of South Africa, the French or British law that ruled the colonies, and the law of Moscow that subordinated all other ethnic groups in the former USSR are examples of that inadequacy.

We get angry too, like Amos and James, about the way the law is applied (Am 2:6–7; Jas 5:4). The dealer of Wall Street and the shoplifter from a slum, the university graduate and the inner-city primary school drop-out, the person whose skin matches the majority and the member of a minority group are treated differently. Anger has provoked revolts of the poor, from the uprising of the slaves of Spartacus in Rome (71 B.C.E.) to the one of the peasants in Luther's Germany (1524–26), right up to the riots of Los Angeles (1992). The anger often aims at the leaders of institutions like nations, unions, churches, or parties, who have little concern for the poor — like Pilate and the Sanhedrin who had no interest in Jesus' rights.

These authorities often give priority to their institution and whatever they claim to safeguard: the Proletariat in the ex-communist countries, racial purity in Nazi Germany, freedom for the French revolution, dogma and Scripture during the Reformation. In the Passion, the rights of the poor man Jesus were sacrificed for the good of Israel and for the Roman order. Like Jesus, the powerless are crushed, especially if they rebel. That Chinese student who faced down the army tanks in Tiananmen Square (Beijing, 1989) counted for nothing, for no more than Jesus before the power of the Sanhedrin and of the Roman Empire.

Do we need another reason for our anger? The passions of today often come down to the same issue as in Jesus' Passion: It's a matter of money. Victims, urged on by representatives of the media, sell the rights to the drama they experienced. The Churches sold the relics of the martyrs; the high priests invested the "blood money" in a field (Mt 27:6–10). Our anger has a real basis and is supported by Jesus' words. We can apply his judgment in Matthew 25 to leaders. He condemns those who refuse to care for the hungry and the thirsty, the foreigner and the naked, the sick and the prisoner: "In so far as you neglected to do this to one of the least of these, you neglected to do it to me" (Mt 25:45). And in Matthew 26, Jesus becomes one of "the least of these," destroyed by the authorities. Jesus did not give in to anger, but it is understandable that others do, and we among them, when the powerless are sacrificed.

Some people, whether or not they are the actual victims, demand the punishment of the guilty party. No question, a society must protect the common good by punishing those who attack it. But in an ethical improvement the Old Testament limited the punishment: The law of retaliation forbids subjecting a criminal to a punishment more severe than what the victim had suffered (Ex 21:24; Dt 19:21). Still today some victims don't have this sense of restraint and demand more punishment for the criminal than what had been inflicted. Others are still "in" the

Old Testament in demanding tit for tat. These people add more violence to the crime that affected them, the violence toward the criminal that gnaws at their hearts, often springing from hidden motives that are not always praiseworthy. While guaranteeing the social order, a Christian is required to go further than tit for tat, because Jesus did not ask God for the kind of retaliation we like.

I have already talked about Jesus' nonviolence. I simply add that he had asserted, "It was said, 'Eye for eye and tooth for tooth.... But on the contrary, if anyone hits you on the right cheek, offer him *another* as well" (Mt 5:38–39). Literally, the text does not say "the other cheek," but "another." I agree with scholars who see here an appeal to refuse the *same* cycle of violence, an invitation to find *another* answer. The revenge that some victims demand perpetuates the violence of the original crime. Countries that have abolished capital punishment have understood that *it is violence* — even though it is legal. On January 25, 1993, the U.S. Supreme Court ruled that death-row prisoners presenting a belated evidence of their innocence have no right to be heard by a federal court. Dissenting Justice Harry A. Blackmun even said, "The execution of a person who can show that he is innocent comes perilously close to simple murder."

Crime provokes our anger and demands punishment. This is understandable, for wherever a crime is committed we are somehow all the victims. The world still feels the rebounds of the Nazi atrocities. Our fear of going into the city at night is evidence that crime affects all of us. One child gets kidnapped and all parents worry. Every attack on a member of any minority group is a threat since we can all be in the minority somewhere, sometime. Our anger is normal, say some people, and especially when the victim is a powerless person or an innocent party. Are we just as angry about the Passion of Jesus? What would we have done if we had been present?

For what do we do when this Passion is repeated to-

day? We are passive, focused on our own interests without
making any effort to correct what promotes crime. Often
leaders of institutions don't set an example because they
fear our selfish reactions, as members of unions, parties,
churches, or a nation. We complain, but at the same time
we support the games of the society that hurt us. We accept the sale of guns without any control; when a domestic
dispute results in the death of an innocent bystander, what
can we say? If we tolerate the rejection of refugees by our
government, can we complain when we ourselves become
undesirables? If we do not give the powerless a voice, let
us keep still on the day our society refuses to listen to
us. If we are too lazy to vote, let us not complain about
the impact of our government's decisions on our life, etc.
Jesus was also the victim of the inertia and the cowardice
of some Jews. The night he was condemned, where were
Joseph of Arimathea and Nicodemus, members of the Sanhedrin? The weak attempt by Nicodemus to defend Jesus
in John 7:50-52 seems insufficient.

So we are all more or less victims because we are all
guilty. Guilty, we want God to adopt our law, judgment,
and injustice. Victims, we expect God to espouse our bitterness and desire for revenge. If God were to act this way
we would be unfortunate indeed since we are all guilty.
"There is no just person, not even one!" (Rom 1-3; Ps
14:3; 53:4). Fortunately, the God of Jesus accepts our feelings with respect but does not follow in our ways (Is 55:8-
9). When the adulterous woman is brought before him,
Jesus teaches us that God does not act like we do: Love
does not excuse, judge, or condemn the sinner (Jn 8:1-11).
Love loves. Ask the parents of any criminal.

When we are before God, victims as well as guilty, we
hear Jesus say, "Always treat others as you would like them
to treat you" (Mt 7:12). But especially in the Passion the
God of Jesus teaches us *another* way than our ways. God
knows the best way for the individual and the group in the
long run: *forgiveness.*

Jesus asks that *every* victimized Christian *always* forgive. This is the meaning of the "seventy times seven times" (Mt 18:22). In his prayer we ask to be forgiven "as we forgive those who have sinned against us" (Mt 6:12). Jesus' invitation to forgive is unconditional. It is often expressed in very strong words, "Love your enemies and pray for those who persecute you" (Mt 5:44). Even though "love" in the New Testament means "serve" and not necessarily "like," Jesus' words are firm. We have no choice. Jesus' call is final. The trial of Jesus, which never led to any revenge on his part, is our trial when we are victimized — not when we cannot forgive, for God understands our weakness, but when we don't even *want* to forgive. Jesus, himself a victim, showed us the example. "Father, forgive them; they do not know what they are doing," he prayed before dying (Lk 23:34). And many martyrs have followed him, starting with Stephen (Acts 7:60).

Jesus in his trial shows us a God far from our usual notions. This God leads us further than the legalistic purity of the scribes and Pharisees. The Gospels never mention any lawyer defending Jesus: Can we be advocates for the innocent and powerless of our time? But can we also, while assuring the needs of justice, be advocates of compassion and mercy toward the guilty people who wrong us? Can we become a part of the solution since we have already been part of the problem? At the time of Augustine, some who suffered martyrdom interceded for apostates who wanted to come back into the Church. After the Vietnam war, some veterans interceded for deserters. Every democracy has statutes of limitations and policies that guarantee amnesty. Can't we be more just but at the same time more merciful and forgiving?

We may say, "I am not strong enough for that." But the Spirit of Jesus' Love can accomplish in us much more than we would believe. Jesus guaranteed that: "I tell you most solemnly, whoever believes in me will perform the same works as I do myself, and will perform even greater works," and, "For people this is impossible; for God everything is possible" (Jn 14:12; Mt 19:26).

History has seen many times true justice, a justice that does not discriminate, a justice that forgives. We must honor those judges who dared to apply the law to the rich and powerful, sometimes at the cost of their lives. I think of Paolo Borsellino and Giovanni Falcone, assassinated in Italy because of their struggle against the Mafia (1992). We must be grateful for prosecutors who had the courage to refrain from demanding the maximum punishment when it was not indicated, who dared to ask for a merciful judgment. We must rejoice in those lawyers who defend with the same diligence both the rich and the poor; in those who seriously defended their clients in countries where a dictator or public opinion or a church prevented true justice. We must exalt all those victims who never sought revenge and who have forgiven.

Years ago, in California, an adolescent killed his girlfriend. The judge accepted the proposal of the girl's parents to keep the murderer with them because they still loved him. They had forgiven and wanted to help him.

Yes, we must hold in memory all of those anonymous people fighting for justice and for human rights, particularly those who fight on behalf of the powerless. Thousands have been tortured or assassinated or have disappeared, in South America, for example. In their Passion, these men and women tell us something about the God of Jesus in his Passion. And when they forgave, this God shone even more through them. They are God with us. They save us.

I'll conclude with a story. A friend of mine, a young nun, died in a car accident in 1980. She had been raped three years before that. I met with her shortly after the rape. After hours of listening I left her saying, "Remember that someday you will have to forgive him." As I suggested, she pressed charges and the rapist was arrested. The man was somewhat mentally handicapped and had raped four other women, one of whom had become pregnant. This woman's husband refused to believe she had been raped. My friend helped all of them, and the husband ended up believing his wife. One day my friend and this couple went to visit the rapist in prison in order to urge him to get treatment. He asked them to forgive him, and they did. And, on top of that, when the rapist had finished his prison term, the husband gave him a job in his business.

The Trials: In the Courtyard—
The Trial of the Churches*

I N THE PASSION ACCOUNTS the trial sequence is the
longest part. This indicates the importance of what is
going on before the Sanhedrin and Pilate. But three evangelists, especially John, mingle Peter's denial with the trial
before the Sanhedrin. There is more to this than just two
events that occur at the same time. I see a suggestion
here that what takes place out in the courtyard is another
trial. Matthew, Mark, and Luke repeat the name of Peter,
a name used to designate Simon as the first apostle, on
whom the Church was built (Mt 16:18). John uses both
"Peter" and "Simon-Peter," apparently recalling the human
weakness of the one denying his Master. This suggests that
the scene of the denial is the trial of the Church and its
fragile leaders. And the Church speaks repeatedly of Peter's
denial in both its founding texts and in its liturgies. Few
social organizations dare do that. Many Germans would
like to forget Hitler and many Russians Stalin; some Americans would rather obliterate the memory of Nixon and
Watergate. The Church is not ashamed of the fault of its
first apostle.

But it is easier to recall an old story than to remember
that the same thing is going on now. All the disciples left

---

*Mt 26:58–75; Mk 14:54–72; Lk 22:54–62; Jn 18:15–27.

Jesus except the few present on Golgotha. So we can assume that Peter, who on one hand symbolizes the leaders, also symbolizes the new People of God. By suggesting this, the Church includes in Peter's denials all the denials that the Church itself and its leaders have committed during two thousand years. What happens in that outer courtyard is the culmination of all the admonitions made to the leaders of the Church so frequently in the Gospels (and of the ones we find in the Old Testament, for instance, in Ezekiel 34).

Peter *is* the priest and the Levite who ignore their brother who lies wounded in a ditch, though we would have expected them to be compassionate because of their ministry (Lk 10:29–37). But here we no longer have a mere parable; this is what happens to a real man. Peter repeats, "I do not know the man." Poor Jesus, stripped of his titles, name, and true identity. He is reduced to the minimum, the man, the human being that he is. He becomes a simple negligible unit among the millions of human beings on earth. He is just another statistic, we would say today. And this annihilation is done by one of those who knew him best (Ps 55:13–15). There have always been, everywhere, numerous lay people, ministers, and leaders who have witnessed to the Gospel — Dietrich Bonhoeffer in Nazi Germany, Martin Luther King, Jr. in the United States, and Archbishop Oscar Romero in El Salvador, for instance. But the legions of heroes, well-known or anonymous, cannot erase the denials of many others in the Church.

Often in history, church leaders have ignored those who suffer, while these poor people were hoping for another example from them. Here are a few examples: the silence of many Latin American bishops about thousands of people who disappeared under the dictatorships of the 1970s; the silence of most French bishops about the Jews' fate during the German occupation of France (1940–45); the silence of some of them, from 1954 to 1960, about the torture practiced in Algeria by the French troops; the silence of many church leaders about their ministers who molested children. "I do not know what you are talking about," Peter says in their name. How many innocent people have been reduced to nothing — a statistic of suffering and death, by the ill will of the heads of the Church. But we have seen worse.

The Churches have assassinated one another. Like the brigands in Jesus' parable, they wounded and killed their brothers and sisters, either socially by excommunication or physically by executing them (Lk 10:30). Reciprocal persecutions have piled up the corpses of those who died in fidelity to their faith! The conflict in Northern Ireland between Protestants and Catholics is one of these examples today, even if the basis for this antagonism is really social. In 1973 a Baptist minister in Kentucky welcomed me saying, "You are the first priest in my life with whom I am shaking hands." Centuries earlier we would have slit one another's throats in Christ's name, sure we were being faithful to him! Christians have murdered believers of other religions as well, Jews in Europe and animists in Africa or America.

Other religions are not any different. The conflicts between the Sunnis and the Shiites in Iraq, between Muslims and Hindus in India, the anger of orthodox Jews about all the others in Israel are some examples. The spirit of crusade is not dead! Only the names of the victims change with the time and the place. Here the Jews or the people of color, there the Christians or the homosexuals. The ravages of religious fanatics on the poor, often guided by their leaders, are endless — as infinite as God's sorrow. If an artist of today were to paint again the famous medieval fresco "The Danse Macabre," one would see rabbis and popes, monks and imams, bonzes and bishops, along with their civil counterparts, taking hold of one another's hands and tragically tripping off to Hell.

The same fanaticism moved the Churches to persecute *their own* innocent members. A Jesuit priest I knew died because he had been destroyed emotionally by the pope's decision to end the worker-priest experiment in France (1953). Each religious group has had its own Inquisitions, persecuted its Galileos, and killed its Joans of Arc. While committing these atrocities within their own ranks, each religion has carried on its murderous exterior crusades. Political leaders never invented racist discourse; the Churches have created it, and in God's name. Jesus' lamentation is addressed to all these institutions and their leaders: "Jerusalem, Jerusalem, you that kill the prophets and stone those who are sent to you" (Mt 23:37). We understand what one of my atheist friends said to me: "On the day the Churches canonize the innocent people they have martyred, then I will believe in them!"

Interestingly, Luke and John have Peter deny Jesus with the words, "I am not [one of Jesus' followers]." At the moment he is recognized as one of the disciples, he is not one any longer. By denying the Son of Man, he is no longer one with those who must love one another (Jn 13:34–35; 15:10–15). No matter what his reasons are, he denies Jesus the Poor One, Love in human flesh; he fails in his own love, in his own human flesh. Many leaders have repeated his sin against the Innocent. But we would have a lot of nerve to condemn them. They have often acted like this because their supporters, and we among them, went along with their denials and even pushed them to crush the scapegoats of the time. We can't cast the first stone because, at our level, we have also denied whoever was the victim of the moment. How many times have we implied by our words, actions, and silences, when faced with a suffering human being, "I do not know this one?" Each time we did this, we denied love in our flesh; we were no longer the disciples of Jesus.

Some people would say, "Yes, but our denials don't have the same dimensions as the denials of our leaders." Indeed, people who are in charge have more power and so their faults carry more impact than ours. However, we must recognize with honesty that we are all leaders in one way or another compared with the powerless: parents with their children, teachers with students, eldest siblings with the youngest, educated people with the unlearned, the rich with the poor, the healthy with the sick. Peter symbolizes each one of us in the measure that we each possess even a small amount of leadership and still deny our brothers or our sisters. We have to admit that we are sinners. But if we claim our "right" to be sinners, let us give that "right" also to our leaders. If we believe that we can be forgiven, they can be forgiven as well.

This brings us to the depth of Peter's denial. Why does he deny *three times*? Aside from the theatrical effect that makes us hope for a change of attitude and reinforces our disappointment each time he repeats his sin, this figure tells us something else. This *three* is like the *three* days of the Passion, where Jesus plunges into his death. Peter, in his denial, and we in ours, plunge into the death of love. Yet, the three days are not a dead end; they open out into a new life for the risen Jesus. The triple denial of Peter prepares the ground for a complete reversal of the situation, which immediately appears: Peter weeps out of sadness and repentance. Peter is overcome with contrition, which is the condition for forgiveness, forgiveness that is an opening to life, a new chance for love. Peter will not be subjected to God's anger, but to pardon. Meanwhile, through him and through his fault, God will perform another astonishing work.

In Luke, Jesus predicts this paradoxical action of God toward Peter, "Simon, Simon! Remember that Satan has asked for you, to sift you like wheat. But I have prayed for you that your faith may never fail. You in turn must strengthen your brothers" (Lk 22:31–32). Our God is a powerful and creative love that can transform everything, even the worst. Out of Peter, the renegade, God makes the rock on which is built the Church, even as from the crime of the crucifixion God made the instrument of our salvation (Mt 16:18). I have spoken about this creative anger and revolt of God in my book *May I Hate God?* God, who is even more of a genius than Picasso, creates a masterpiece out of scrap metal — just as we do when we learn to profit from our mistakes. A lot of Alcoholics Anonymous members and prisoners have extracted from their failed past a new and fruitful life.

Certain church leaders have experienced this kind of "reversal of fortune." Archbishop Romero of El Salvador is a good example of this change. From the conservative that he was, he became an ardent defender unto death of the poor and innocent victims of his country. This is the reason that the Church has never hesitated to hold up before us the weakness of its leader, Peter. If the Church insists on reminding us of his denial, it is no doubt to call its leaders to humility. But it is for another reason even more important. The Church asserts that it is in Peter that the infinite mercy of God, who pardons the repentant sinner, is manifest. Through Peter's weakness, God's power of love "is made perfect" (2 Cor 12:9). This is the unheard of creativity of Love, who draws out of what sin had made a grace even more astounding. Paul, who knew personally this power of God through Christ, says, "But where sin abounded, grace did much more abound" (Rom 5:20).

Believing in such a power, let's hope for the same conversion for all leaders. All of them, all of us. May we not stay out in the cold like Peter did that night. At the very least, let's wish that all of us, having fully realized our denials, might one day *weep*.

"Ecce Homo"

I N THE MIDDLE of John's account of the Passion, we hear a short but terrible phrase that invites us to look at an awful Jesus. For centuries that phrase has touched many hearts. It does the same for us today because of what we see there. Pilate shows Jesus to the leaders of Israel and to the crowd, saying once more that he does not find him guilty. However, he has had Jesus scourged. Maybe he thought that a minimum of punishment would awaken pity in the hearts of Jesus' enemies and prevent further persecution of that poor preacher. He says, "Ecce Homo. Here is the man" (Jn 19:5).

We can imagine how Jesus looks after hours of sufferings. He has been hurt in his heart. The ones he loves have abandoned and betrayed him. He has been mocked, insulted, and ridiculed by his adversaries and their accomplices. And, all the while, most of the people of Jerusalem ignore his fate; at this moment, they are having their breakfast and going quietly off to their daily business. Why would they worry about some man who might get the death penalty and be executed? And the worst part of it is that he is condemned, unjustly, by the leaders of his own "Church," the Synagogue.

He has also suffered in his body. I won't insist on this aspect of his sufferings, as some preachers do, because the Gospels don't. The Gospels do not depict the pornography of bloody violence that fascinates some of us. But we need to remember a few details: No food, no drink for hours; he has been beaten up and scourged.

> So marred was his look beyond that of man, and his appearance beyond that of mortals.... There was in him no stately bearing to make us look at him. He was spurned and avoided by people, a man of suffering, accustomed to infirmity. One of those from whom people hide their faces, spurned, and we held him in no esteem... like a lamb led to the slaughter or a sheep before the shearers, he was silent and opened not his mouth. (Is. 52:13–53:12)

Here we have a Jesus nobody likes to look at.

"Here is the man," says Pilate. Christians have heard, "Here is the Human Being." Before *that* Jesus we can confess our personal and collective sins against human beings, because this is the way we treat Love in our flesh, because this is the way we treat our brothers and sisters, ourselves. Contemplating Jesus, there, invites us to look at what we, collectively, do to others. We have abandoned and betrayed, excluded and condemned, or ignored them. We have injured or killed them. It is for each one of us to remember what we have done, individually and collectively. We have abandoned allies when it was no longer to our advantage to remain on their side. We, the rich, have abandoned poor nations to their fate, because they had no oil or mineral resources that we could exploit. We have also killed. In Hiroshima, Japan, and in Germany after World War II we wonder, "How many innocent people have paid the price of our wars?" We could make a long list of events like these right up to our present day. We usually don't like to be reminded of our actions or to see pictures of their results. This is a "Jesus nobody likes to look at," as I wrote above. Yes, we do not like to look at our victims.

We continue to do the same here and now. We easily abandon the homeless and jobless when we rebel against taxes used for social programs. While we breakfast or go

quietly about our daily business we ignore thousands of
children who, in many countries, are "deprived of basic
health care, shelter, food, and safe environment" (according to an official report about Connecticut in 1992, when
the state ranked first for personal income in the United
States!).

In the face of *that* Jesus, we might at least stop treating
the human beings closest to us badly. I knew a pregnant
woman who was rejected by her family because she was
not married to the father of her unborn child. I knew another who was shut out by her relatives because she chose
to live with an ex-prisoner. I know some people who have
been treated as outcasts and persecuted because they were
gay or lesbian or they had had an abortion. On a social
level, we hurt, exclude, condemn, ignore, or destroy some
human beings.

"Here is the Human Being." But this disfigured Christ
is also each one of us. Each time we injure another human
being we damage ourselves. We amputate ourselves, one
limb of the human body. To exclude somebody else is to
exclude ourselves from what they could bring to us; we are
the ones who pay the price. One good example of this is
our penal system. Because we refuse to correct the social
ills of our nation, we have an increasing number of prisoners, and we pay the price through our taxes. This is an
amputation! The money taken out of our income is gone,
and the skills and capacities of inmates are wasted behind
the bars of the correctional institutions.

"Here is the Human Being!" We also mistreat ourselves.
We ignore or injure our own bodies, minds, and hearts.
Our addictions damage all three of these aspects of ourselves because we don't nourish them correctly. All we
have to do is look at the kind of food we eat, the readings
or TV we feed our minds, and the fantasies and dreams
consumed by our hearts. We are a junk-food society fasci-
nated by violence and soap operas, and yet we are surprised
when our children are fat or behave erratically.

We must include here the lessons from ecology. The International Conference of Rio de Janeiro (1992) demonstrated the resistance of many governments to taking the steps necessary to save the earth. We are not just on earth, we are made of it; it's a part of us. What we do to this planet comes back to us like a boomerang. Acid rain, nuclear waste, pollution of water, destruction of the forests and of endangered species, and other human plagues disfigure us. Moreover, our continual aggression toward the planet promises wounds in the future for our own children and grandchildren. The ten plagues of Egypt are repeated, but this time they are the direct result of our own actions, and they will wipe out more than just our firstborn (Ex 7–11). In a less obvious way, perhaps, we wound and kill when we waste, vandalize, or procrastinate maintenance. The food that we waste and the monuments that we efface were produced out of hours of work and sweat, out of the lives of other human beings. To waste and vandalize is to mistreat the human lives that were transformed into these consumable or admirable products. Also, bridges collapse, trains are derailed, fire engines or school buses crash, and people are injured or killed because of poor maintenance.

Through all of that, we deface our own beauty at the deepest level of our humanity, for we wound our capacity of love through our human flesh. If another becomes a disfigured Christ through our actions, it is because we have first marred Love within our own hearts. Love is suffering and bleeding in the child of God we all are because of our own faults. Thus, when we look at the disfigured Son of God in human flesh that Pilate shows us, we are contemplating *ourselves*. Here we are, injured human beings present in this One, two thousand years ago. As I said earlier, before the Jesus brought out by Pilate to show us, we must confess both our individual and collective sin.

However, even though all of that is extremely important, because it is a question of life and death for humanity, the main revelation in what we contemplate is *not* all that I have described. Undoubtedly we must recognize and own our sins, be sorry for what we have done and are still doing, and enter into a sincere conversion of heart and change of behavior. But God, through Jesus, is not primarily interested in revealing our sins. The Incarnation did not occur because of our sins (as some old theologies used to teach) but because God wanted to reveal Love. The whole Bible, and the words and actions of Jesus in particular, is first of all the revelation of God's love for us; it is the Revelation of Love. And Jesus is still that Revelation when Pilate brings him out of the praetorium.

"Here is the man, Jesus." From his mouth *we don't hear one single word.* "Like a lamb led to the slaughter..., he was *silent* and opened not his mouth," Isaiah had said (Is 53:7; Ps 38:14–15). Of course, some people would wonder, "What *can* you say when you have been tortured emotionally and physically, and when you are facing your enemies and the rage of a crowd?" But the fact is that not one word of complaint or revenge, blame or anger, judgment or condemnation comes out of Jesus' mouth. None. Our being often takes revenge when we have injured it: Our body gets sick, our mind no longer functions, and our heart hurts. People too often take revenge when we have hurt them, and we have done the same thing to others, blaming them angrily, condemning them because of the wounds they have inflicted on us. But from God's human mouth there were none of those harsh reactions and bitter words. Only a silence. It is impossible to imagine God enjoying what had been done to Jesus, but God did not complain or take revenge, did not blame us out of anger or condemn us through him. Ironically enough, God is not even trying to make us feel guilty in the Passion, as some preachers do.

This is the kind of God we perceive once in a while through powerful experiences. Parents have suffered silently from the behavior of their children. Friends have refused to express their emotional sufferings caused by one another's behavior. They did not appreciate what was happening. It caused them to agonize, but they went on loving, and so does God. God can seem silent in our lives sometimes, often because of what we are doing to others and ourselves, but God still loves us.

Someone I know had been condemned and rejected by some friends — after thirty years of presumed friendship — because of a decision she had made. The first time she met them again, her first reaction was to ask them genuinely about their own worries and joys and to listen to them. She never said a word about what they had done to her. Silent about all of her pain, she loved them again through her attention. So does Love, so does God with us.

"Here is Jesus, here is God," innocent and hurt by our behavior, but loving us. "I speak no more, since you yourself are at work," says the psalm (Ps 39:9). Silent, but *still* there as an unconditional Love. This is the revelation we must keep in our mind and cherish in our heart. To let the contemplation of such Love in such a Jesus sink into ourselves is healing. "All you who pass this way, look and see; is any sorrow like the sorrow that afflicts me?" (Lam 1:12). If our hearts are not callous, if they are hearts of flesh and not stony hearts, what we see at the gate of the praetorium is going to find an echo within us (Ez 36:26). When we experience sorrow for our sins, this is already a sign that God's Love within us answers God's Love seen "here, in this man, Jesus."

*Barabbas**

THIS JESUS whom Pilate presents to the crowd is the sorrowful icon created by our sins when we do violence to ourselves or others. The four evangelists give us another symbol that might explain the underlying logic of this drama, of our daily drama and of the reaction of God. Just before saying, "Here is the man," and just after the final condemnation of Jesus, Pilate makes a decision concerning another prisoner, Barabbas.

Many Christians have been struck by what happens to this man during the Passion of Jesus. A "notorious prisoner," a "robber," he was in jail because he had "committed a murder during an insurrection." That's all we know about his past, but it is clear that, for the evangelists, he is a "bad guy." He was probably one of those people who solve their problems by resorting to violence. We don't know anything about the rest of his life either, except that he becomes a free man. When his path is accidentally bisected by that of Jesus, he wins his liberty in spite of the charges weighing against him.

Pilate appears not to want to condemn Jesus and seems to employ a strategy to save him. He makes use of the custom of liberating a prisoner for the Passover. He proposes that the Jews choose between Jesus "who is called Christ" and Barabbas. The priests and the elders persuade the crowd and they shout, "Not this man, but Barabbas!"

*Mt 27:15–23; Mk 15:6–14; Lk 23:17–23; Jn 18:39–40.

104

Barabbas serves then as a foil to Jesus' being. For they choose the violent one over the gentle one, the criminal rather than the innocent one, the one who killed before the Messiah who saves (Mt 11:29). This is the same choice that is at the basis of our own behavior much of the time. As I said in the previous chapter, we choose violence, and we ourselves or others pay the price, and sometimes the innocent pay — like our descendants.

A French author, René Girard, in his book *Violence and the Sacred** developed a thesis illustrated here: Every society is a hotbed of tension that festers and secretes violence. When the tension becomes intolerable, then the people join together against a scapegoat, supposedly guilty of everything, and they destroy him or her. Once this is done, the social group enjoys a respite from tension in the (false) communion afforded by the preparation and the accomplishment of the destruction of the accused. But because the outcome is a violence, it engenders new disagreements and very soon the violent cycle repeats itself. René Girard sees Jesus as the cultural model for Westerners that breaks the vicious circle. We don't find in Jesus an attempt to lay on another scapegoat the violence oppressing him. Rather, he absorbs the violence aimed at him and, by so doing, destroys it. Violence cannot go further, annihilated in Jesus' forgiveness. And his disciples will be invited to do the same "seventy times seven times" (Mt 18:21). Jesus saves us from violence by his behavior, if we choose him.

We are continually faced with the choice between Barabbas or Jesus "who is called Christ" (Mt 27:17, 22). Choosing Barabbas is the option that gives free reign to violence perpetrated against a scapegoat in us or around us. Choosing Jesus, the Paschal Lamb, is to try to absorb the violence and to save, with him, like him. As I said in the chapters about violence, this is not submission out of weakness; it

---

*Baltimore: Johns Hopkins University Press, 1977.

is the opposite! After having done everything to find a remedy for violence, we drown it by an overflow of love whose most magnificent proof is forgiveness. This might include suffering. It's the kind of painful victory that those who have truly forgiven have experienced. Those who can forgive save society. We have the equivalent at the national or international level. Many people from both the North and the South did everything they could to avoid the Civil War in 1861. Once the war was over many became the instruments of reciprocal forgiveness in order to repair the unity of the nation. France, Great Britain, and the United States attempted several diplomatic strategies in order to avoid the war with Germany and Japan at the end of the 1930s; now these two countries, forgiven, are allies.

All of this is precious enough, but the meeting of Jesus and Barabbas reveals other surprising things about the God of the Gospels. One day Jesus cured a woman without her having asked him for anything. Gratuitously, he released her "from her shackles," from the "bondage" she had known for eighteen years (Lk 13:10–17). In the same way, in his Passion, Jesus liberated Barabbas even though he never asked him for freedom and never did anything to deserve this grace. We might wonder why God acted in this way, just like we can wonder why God would one day liberate a Saul to become Paul. Subtly, the Gospel texts tell us the reason for such a grace and mercy.

For any Jewish ear the name Bar-abbas meant, "Son of Abba," for that's its meaning for many scholars. We remember the blind man, Timaeus' son, Bar-timaeus, in Mark 10, for instance (46–52). But "Abba" is the name chosen by Jesus to address God (Mk 14:30). This is the tender, trustful, and spontaneous name that children use with their father: Dad, Daddy. The Gospel writers are telling us that this Bar-Abbas, this robber and murderer is *also*, is *still* the son of a God we must trust and love as a very tender dad. "If you with all your sins know how to give your children what is good, how much more will your heavenly father give good things to anyone who asks him," said Jesus (Mt 7:11). Here the Father acts according to Jesus' word and goes even further, because he totally liberates one of his sons, though this murderer never even asked, according to what the Gospels tell us. This is accomplished because of the other son, Jesus. For "God did not send the Son into the world to condemn the world, but that the world might be saved through him" (Jn 3:17). God liberates Barabbas freely because of the beloved Son Jesus. We are sons and daughters of God, often other violent Barabbases, but we too can hope in God's mercy because God cannot act otherwise since Jesus.

In fact, what is going on here is not so strange at all to those Christians who were former Jews. They already knew something about that mercy from the time of Genesis: Back then one of Barabbas' violent ancestors, and one of ours, killed his brother Abel. In Cain the whole history of brotherly violence begins. But what a surprise for us when we see how God answers Cain's complaint, "My punishment is greater than I can bear. See! Today you drive me from this ground. I must hide from you, and be a fugitive and a wanderer over the earth. Whoever comes across me will kill me!" Sure, God did ask Cain, "Where is your brother Abel? What have you done?" But God promises, "Not so! If anyone kills Cain, Cain shall be avenged sevenfold." And "the Lord put a mark on Cain, lest anyone should kill him at sight" (Gn 4:9–15). God refuses the spiral of violence that Cain's act might have created and protects the murderer. But the belief that God preserves and saves human beings because of *sonship* (theologians would say) takes on in Jesus a deeper dimension because of the Incarnation.

A copyist of the past has added a word to Matthew 27:17. In a few versions of a manuscript referred to as "Caesarean," the verse reads, "Whom do you want me to release for you, *Jesus*-Bar-Abbas or Jesus-called-Christ?" (hyphens are mine). Maybe the person who altered the text wanted to give us a key to the mystery of God's mercy toward all sons and daughters, even violent murderers like Barabbas. Since the Incarnation, human beings like you and me have not always been saviors for others — *Christ*-like (the word "Christ" translates into Greek the Hebrew word *Messiah:* Savior). In spite of that, we are always *Jesus*-like because of the Spirit within us (the word "Jesus," in the New Testament, means very often just the man of Nazareth). When we are no longer saviors, we are still a "Jesus-Bar-Abbas," a Jesus son of Abba.

After all, many mothers and fathers have said to their son or daughter in prison, without excusing the crime, "You have not served others. You have even killed them. But you are *still* my child." If we are capable of such love, why not God?

Jesus Crucified *

I DON'T CALL THIS CHAPTER "the cross." Too many
Christians are focused on the cross. The Gospel is not
about an instrument of execution, but about Jesus. And on
Golgotha, the Gospel still invites us to look at the God
who is revealed in this crucified Jesus. The insistence on
the cross has promoted a theology of suffering that dis-
torts Christian revelation and justifies sado-masochism on
both a personal and group level. According to this perspective, the more people suffer the more truly Christian
they are (while sometimes our sufferings are nothing more
or less than the natural outcome of our own mistakes).
This trial was "God's will"; God must have willed this
suffering and death of the Son! Many people have been re-
volted by this idea. Elie Wiesel on the subject of Isaac "tied
up" (translated incorrectly sometimes as "the sacrifice of
Isaac") wrote this:

> In passing, we should mention the role played by this
> scene in Christianity: The threat hanging over Isaac is
> seen as a prefiguration of the crucifixion. Except that
> on Mount Moriah the act was *not* consummated: The
> father did *not* abandon his son. Such is the distance
> between Moriah and Golgotha. In Jewish tradition
> man cannot use death as a means of glorifying God.
> Every man is an end unto himself, a living eternity;

*Mt 27:32–66; Mk 15:21–47; Lk 23:26–56; Jn 19:16–30, 38–42.

no man has the right to sacrifice another, not even to God.... For the Jew, all truth must spring from life, never from death. To us, crucifixion represents not a step forward but a step backward: at the top of Moriah, the living remains alive, thus marking the end of an era of ritual murder. To invoke the *Akeda* [the name refers to what happened to Isaac on Mount Moriah] is tantamount to calling for mercy — whereas from the beginning Golgotha has served as pretext for countless massacres of sons and fathers cut down together by sword and fire in the name of a word that considered itself synonymous with love. Let us now close the parentheses and follow Abraham.*

And this is my point exactly: A healthy theology sees in the One who was crucified the ultimate word about Love, about God. Imagine that you are at the bedside of your best friend who, having just saved your life by risking her own, lies suffering and dying. The way you would look at her is the same way we should contemplate Jesus crucified. For us Christians, the Incarnation is the mystery of God-Trinity deciding to send the Second Person among us, in order to come to our rescue, to love us, and to reveal what Love is about. Jesus is the revelation and the expression of that absolutely free and unconditional God-Love. This is a Love that nothing can stop if only we will open the door — a Love at any cost, a Love ready to pay any price. It is *we* human beings, and not God, *who have made* the cross the price of that Love — through those who condemned Jesus. Just like any mother or father, God could *never* will the cross for the Son. But God does want to love, in Jesus, even to the point of accepting crucifixion by us.

This has been our experience. We may freely decide we will love someone, but it is *always* the other who decides, by his or her response to our love, the price we will have to

---

*Elie Wiesel, *Messengers of God: Biblical Portraits and Legends* (New York: Summit Books, 1976), p. 76 (from *Célébrations Bibliques* [Paris: Seuil, 1975]).

pay. We have been crucified by those people we loved who have repaid us poorly; in our turn, we have crucified the ones who loved us when our response brought them pain. But when, though wounded in our love, we have remained steadfast, we have seen, in our own lives, the same mystery that we see in Jesus crucified — someone loving until the end (Jn 13:1).

Maybe this is one of the meanings of the "wine... mingled with gall" or "myrrh" that is offered to Jesus. Historians say that this drink would anesthetize the person being crucified so that he would not feel the pain. In Matthew and Mark, Jesus refuses this drink. Perhaps his refusal expressed his desire to pay the whole price that we had exacted without holding anything back. Or maybe he wanted to stay consciously present to everything and everybody, as some patients do when they refuse too much of an analgesic. In John, Jesus drinks the "vinegar." Water mixed with vinegar was a common drink for Roman soldiers: refreshing in the way lemonade is, but somewhat bitter. Maybe John suggests that Jesus accepted drinking the bitter cup to the dregs. Psalm 69, implied in John's words, is the prayer of someone whose situation is bitter (Ps 69:8, Ps 22). Jesus, and God in him, drank down to the last drop the bitterness of the dereliction inflicted on him because of love. Love has paid the whole bill that *we* have added up and written. Written? Yes. This bill had been written since Psalm 22, which is often cited in the Gospels (Mt 27:34–35; Mk 15:34; Lk 23:34–35).

The bill had already been written, for the first Christians used to read, in that psalm (or in Wis 2), about humanity's permanent aggression toward love. It must have seemed like the very words of that psalm were being realized when the soldiers cast lots for the seamless tunic of Jesus. The story of God-Love, ridiculed by us, didn't start on Golgotha and it does not end there either. Although it is there that it was totally unveiled.

There is a legend that says that the skull we see at the

foot of the cross in so many artists' renditions of Golgotha is Adam's. This legend attests to the ongoing historical
tragedy of love put to death by us. The Jewish tradition
that sees Isaac "tied up" in a place close to Golgotha says
what Elie Wiesel asserts about the Jewish point of view.
But I hope I have corrected what he wrote about the Christian perspective. Yes, we spend our time crucifying Love in
our children, in others, and in ourselves — but that was
never God's will, neither at the time of Abraham nor at the
time of Jesus. If God-Love never willed and would never
want that, we, on the other hand, have always been experts
at crucifixion. The Spanish in their civil war (1936–40),
the North and South Koreans (1950–52), the Ugandans
under Idi Amin (1971–79), the *tontons macoutes* of Duva-
lier (1957–71), the Somali warlords (1992–93) give us just
a few examples of the way we murder our brothers and
sisters.

God's Love respects our freedom perfectly, even when
we kill Jesus. But the God of Abraham and Jesus never
wanted to be glorified in such a murderous way. God never
wanted Golgotha used as a pretext for slaughtering anyone.
God wanted to love till the end, and in Jesus God did not
fail the test we devised. The rest was, and is, the terrible
fruit of our decision.

Jesus says to the women who weep over him, "Do not
weep for me, but weep for yourselves and for your children" (Lk 23:27–31). He's right. It is not appropriate to
cry over Love who remains free and strong under trial. It
would be fitting to weep over ourselves when we crucify
each other and prepare an awful world for our children. But
tears of sorrow demand awareness and contrition. Obviously, Jesus' adversaries don't seem contrite. But they are
aware of what they are doing.

I have already spoken of their desire for a Messiah of
power, a desire that lay behind their mockery. And I also
talked about the way children test their parents. There is
some of that there when, after having cornered Jesus, they

say, "Let the Christ, the King of Israel, come down now from the cross, that we may see and believe" (Mk 15:32). They want the prowess of a superman, so that they can be convinced and confirmed in their views of the Messiah to come. Was this one of Jesus' temptations? What happened in the desert to Jesus authenticates that possibility. "The devil took him on the pinnacle of the temple, and said to him, 'If you are the Son of God, throw yourself down'... [and with the help of the angels, land gracefully in front of everyone]" (Mt 4:5–6). To come down from the cross would certainly have been spectacular and his adversaries would have been satisfied and converted. (Would they?) And we would have been as well. (Would we?)

But what about the victim's dignity? Jesus would have been tortured for the pleasure of a spectacular ending. The crucifixion would have been a bad movie, made by a sadistic God enjoying, through Jesus' sufferings, the divine suspense! And what about our own dignity, our freedom? If Jesus had asked God for such a miracle, and if God had performed it, we would all have had *our freedom violated* by a violent God. "You shall not tempt the Lord your God," Jesus retorted to the demon (Mt 4:7). From the cross he does not tempt God, for he knows that God is too respectful a lover to rape us, even for an apparently good outcome. No one can be forced to love, and God knows that.

If Jesus does tempt God on the cross, it is in this way: "Father, forgive them; for they know not what they do" (Lk 23:34). And yes, here we see a show, but a show of forgiveness. And the climax of that show is in what happens to the one called the "good thief" (Lk 23:39–43). The story illustrates a Love that is never conquered by our criminal behavior. At the last moment, a criminal recognizes the appropriateness of his punishment and appeals to Jesus. Immediately this man, who is a model of contrition, receives forgiveness and a guarantee of eternal life. Since that thief many a condemned person has benefited from God's mercy, even if not ours. We easily forget that our

God, since Jesus, has had something in common with anyone on death row. God willed neither the sacrifice of Isaac
nor that of Jesus nor that of *anyone;* we, we execute our
brother or sister.

And God did not want any sacrifice for Mary, either.
God gave a ram to Abraham so he could keep his son and
enjoy being the father of Isaac. In a gesture of similar re-
placement, God, through Jesus, gives Mary back a son and
keeps her a mother by confiding her to John (Jn 19:26–27).
For Mary, the God of Jesus follows the path of the God
of Abraham, for it is the same God. Therefore, on Golgotha, the Father and the Son, in the same Spirit, did not
ask for the sacrifice of anybody, but they accepted to be *our*
victims.

Finally, there is Jesus' question, "Eloi, Eloi, lema sa-
bachthani? My God, my God, why have you forsaken me?"
(Mk 15:34). As I said in *May I Hate God?* this painful
question gives us the right to express all our distressed
questions to God. God understood and welcomed Jesus'
cry. Of course, we believe that Jesus was perfectly just and
innocent. If God accepted Jesus' question, how much more
ours will be accepted, since God knows more than anybody
that we are so much weaker. So let us dare to ask our questions, because, when we question someone, we expose our
desire to maintain a relationship with him or her. We reveal that we still cherish it. One step further than that,
Jesus says, "My God, My God . . . "

When the onlookers say, "Behold, he is calling Elijah.
. . . Wait, let us see whether Elijah will come to take him
down," their words are dripping with sarcasm (Mk 15:34–
37). In those days it was believed that Elijah would return
before the coming of the Messiah (Mal 3:23). But Elijah
had come, in the person of John the Baptist, announcing
the real Savior, as Jesus himself had said (Mt 11:14). The
Savior has come. Now he is there on the cross, unconditional Love at the price of the sacrifice we have decided, a
Love forgiving the crimes of all, hearing the cries of all, of

you and me, in Jesus crucified. Jesus is not a parenthesis in history; he is God's Answer to us: "I am, the Lord is here" (Ez 48:35).

And now we hear God's cry. "Crying with a loud voice" Jesus "breathed his last," "yielded up," and "gave up his spirit." These words are reminiscent of another scene, the reverse of this one, where God "blew into [Adam's] nostrils the breath of life" (Gn 2:7). This great cry of Jesus is on a scale with the whole of Creation just like his death, which takes on the dimensions of the entire cosmos and of human history itself. The darkness extends over the whole land, the earth actually quakes, boulders split in two, tombs open up, and the dead come back to life in Matthew's Gospel. In Jewish culture these were all images of chaos and new life, of God's action (Ps 18:7–11). So the evangelist affirms that re-creation has begun for all of us, even if only its dark side appears on Golgotha, for God precedes us "by means of a column of cloud" (Gn 1:2–3; Ex 13:21–22). In the death of this indestructible Love God is already breathing new life into us. The veil of the Temple is torn because the remoteness and the mystery of God, the Holy of Holies, is ended — just as the Epistle to the Hebrews will later say.

For the Gospel writers the first sign of this new creation of God is the act of faith of the Roman centurion, "Truly this man was the Son of God!" (Mt 27:54; Mk 15:39). This is particularly striking in Mark, who finishes the Passion in the same way he began his Gospel (Mk 15:39 = 1:1). From the Synagogue God lets the Church be born. At the moment the evangelists wrote, these new Chosen People were for the most part former pagans. "You, who were strangers in the covenant and its promise; you were without hope and without God in the world. But now in Christ Jesus you who once were far off have been brought near through the blood of Christ." This is what Paul, the ex-Jew, would later write to the pagans (Eph 2:12–13).

One person has been sacrificed by us, Jesus. Out of

that, God brings about the reconciliation of *all*, "reconciling both of us [Gentiles and Jews] to God in one body through his cross, which put enmity to death" (Eph 2:16; Rom 5:12–21). The crucified Jesus gives hope because the forces of death expire under the strength of his love, God's Love. We can all now believe that love will conquer all that is mortal around and in us. So the crucified Jesus cannot be the pretext for countless massacres by sword and fire. Because this Jesus is not just a word synonymous with love. He is Love itself, begging us all in the name of the God of Israel and of the nations to be brothers and sisters and asserting that it is possible to be so in human flesh.

*Naked and Pierced but Not Broken**

THE PASSION IS A LOVE STORY, as I said at the beginning of this book. But love stories often have a happy ending. Where is it here? In John 19, we see a corpse hanging on a cross. Probably not nice to look at. As Isaiah said,

> There was in him no stately bearing to make us look at him, nor appearance that would attract us to him. He was spurned and avoided by people, a man of suffering, accustomed to infirmity. One of those from whom people hide their faces, spurned, and we held him in no esteem. Yet it was our infirmities that he bore, our sufferings that he endured.... He was pierced for our offenses, crushed for our sins. Upon him was the chastisement that makes us whole, by his stripes we were healed.... The Lord laid upon him the guilt of us all." (Is 53:2–6)

Yes, we see a corpse, naked and pierced.

Few artists have portrayed the Crucified Jesus naked. We are sensitive about our sexuality, so to be stripped naked by force is humiliating. Many prisoners, Jesus among them, have experienced this form of abasement. Nudity in the Old Testament is often connected with sin.

---

*Jn 19:31–37.

Since Adam and Eve's sin nakedness has exposed the sinful reality of human behavior and provoked fear and shame (Gn 3:10; Ez 23:29; Hos 2:5, 11–12; Na 3:5). "Your nakedness shall be uncovered and your shame be seen," says Isaiah (47:3). The Law forbade us to unveil the origin of our life (Lv 18:20; Ex 20:26: Gn 9:22–23). But as far as God is concerned, our sin involved just the opposite.

In the naked Jesus, *nothing now hides God's holy Truth.* For centuries and during our own lifetime we have sinned, not by unveiling God's nakedness, but by "clothing" God, our Origin, with many disguises. We have made God into a Judge or someone lying in ambush, a demanding Supreme Being or an authoritarian despot or an indifferent lone wolf. These are some of the disguises we put on God because of our education, our fears, our desire to manipulate, or other reasons. We forget that when God appeared visibly among us, it was with the *human* face of Jesus — a God very human, and on the cross a God vulnerable like us, a God who is no longer dangerous. But we knew that from the beginning: In Bethlehem, God appeared through Jesus disarmed as a naked baby, and as disarming as an infant. We see the same God in the Crucified One, totally disarmed and absolutely disarming.

With no disguise, through his nakedness Jesus says to us, "Here I am, entirely emptied of myself for you. I have let you strip me of everything, of my life — though I am the source of Life. Why? Because I have given myself to you to the point of being definitively given up to you." Many parents can say that to their children, many people to their friends.

"Here I am," says Jesus. *"You know everything about me and so about God,* for nothing is hidden. You don't understand? Maybe because it is too much. . . . So behold me. Everything you want to learn about Love is here in all its nakedness."* Thus, Jesus' nakedness is not humiliation, but the unveiling of an amazing Love. Since Adam and Eve, God has often lovingly clothed sinners with a glorious mantel of salvation and justice, as the Prodigal Father did with his younger son who came home (Gn 3:21; Is 61:3, 10; Lk 15:22). Here the Father accepts that his Son, the Just One on the cross, be stripped of his clothes in order to show what loving is all about.

"And now," says Jesus, "I entrust myself to you. You did what you wanted to do with me. Do what you want to do with me again. I am delivered up to your eyes, words, and hands, as vulnerable as a naked person can be. I am Love: You may mock me, insult me, or crucify me wherever you meet me in your life." (And it is true that we act so with Love.) But two people who are in love can be naked with each other, full of trust and without any shame, with the same innocence that Adam and Eve had before their broken union with God (Gn 2:25). This can be our way with Jesus. "I am Love, says Jesus, you may on the other hand look at me with compassion, speak to me with gratitude, hold me with care, love me wherever you encounter me daily." (And it is true that we can really take care of Love in all our encounters with others.)

So on the cross God is not a judge but a victim; someone not in ambush but betrayed by us; not authoritarian but seemingly vanquished; not indifferent but vulnerable. The Father is not demanding but through Jesus has emptied himself for us; God on the cross is a *beggar*, begging for what we can offer because of our gratitude. God is a beggar just as the ones who are vulnerable because they are naked, with no food or roof over their heads, no health or homeland, no freedom or no one to comfort them. God is a beggar as our love is when we don't force others to love us. God is Love for John, Compassion for Meister Eckhart (1 Jn 4:8). On the cross, God is *vulnerability*. We know what that means with the ones we really love, as children or parents, as spouses or friends.

Forever God is vulnerability for us. Forever? This is visible through the pierced side of Jesus. John insists, "This testimony has been given by an eyewitness, and his testimony is true. He tells what he knows is true, so that you may believe." So what do we see, what are we asked to believe? We see the heart of Jesus, the heart of the perfect human being totally open, vulnerable to God, to Love. And this heart is pouring out for God, for Love, its last drops of blood. In Jesus, the heart of every human being — yours, mine — can now love God humanly, can now love others divinely. But this heart is also the heart of the *Son* of God. The human heart of God, totally vulnerable to us, totally open for and to us, pouring out all the possible love, care and tenderness, mercy and compassion, forgiveness and love we can imagine... if we can, down to the last drop of its blood. The heart of God loving us, you and me, so humanly. This is the God we are called to believe in. This is the Love we are called to let exist within ourselves, in order to remove our heart of stone and be given a heart of flesh (Ez 11:19; 36:26).

But this heart of the perfect Human Being and this heart of God are the one and the same heart in Jesus, pierced by the same lance. Lovers carve two hearts on trees with their names on them, pierced by the same arrow. They want to symbolize their everlasting union, their unending covenant. Here we see, in the same wound, in one single heart the perfection of the covenant of God with us through Jesus. Simeon had said to Mary, "A sword will pierce your soul too — so that the secret thoughts of many may be laid bare" (Lk 2:35). Pierced by a lance, Jesus' heart reveals our secret sinful thoughts, but chiefly the most secret thought of God: God has been so divinely and humanly vulnerable in Jesus that what was done is done forever; God is ours forever, we are God's forever in Jesus. God has chosen to be vulnerable forever. May we, in and with Jesus, choose to be vulnerable also with everybody day after day? It is time we do what Paul told us to do, "put on the Lord Jesus Christ" (Rom 13:14; Eph 4:24). It is time to use the words of an old prayer, "Make my heart unto Thine," time to love divinely and humanly.

If we do so we will often bleed but we will be "Wounded Healer[s]," as the title of Henri Nouwen's book expresses so accurately. When we bleed we suffer, but this blood is our life blood. Women know that. It is with reason that the Church saw in the blood and water flowing from Christ's side both the Baptism that introduces us to Life and the Eucharist that nourishes Love. To love requires a vulnerability that is often painful but always life-giving.

He dies of love but "not one of his bones will be broken," says Scripture. Many have seen in the crucified but unbroken body the sacrament of all our enmities overcome once and for all. Enmity between ourselves and God, between the past and the present, between the body and the soul, between brothers and sisters, according to whether we are looking at the vertical body of Jesus or the horizontal plane formed by his arms. It is true that his public life was spent uniting Matthew the collaborator with Simon the rebellious Zealot, the righteous with the sinners of Israel, observance of the Law with fidelity to Love. The early Church enjoyed the unity demanded and achieved by Jesus, "May they all be one," for within this body there was "no longer Jew or Greek, slave or free man, male or female." This visible social unity is experienced mystically in the celebration of the Eucharist, where "all are one in Christ Jesus" (Jn 17:21; Gal 3:28).

We can certainly make a list of all the unions that remain to be accomplished today and are now attainable. In Jesus' body the covenant of a vulnerable God with us *can never be torn apart*, and therefore all other covenants are possible too. "Who will separate us from the love of Christ? Trial, or distress, or persecution, or hunger, or nakedness, or danger, or the sword? ... Neither death nor life, neither angels nor principalities, neither the present nor the future, nor powers, neither height nor depth, nor any other creature, will be able to separate us from the love of God that comes to us in Christ Jesus, our Lord," said Paul to the Romans (8:35–39). If we understand and believe what we see in Jesus' pierced side, we must be able to say the same with our own words. And if we cannot be separated from the Love of God through Christ, can we work with hope against the current separations we still suffer with our brothers and sisters? It has already begun. I knew a woman who kept her husband and their two sons together for ten years while the teenagers were drug addicts. We all remember Gandhi keeping the members of many different religions together until India became independent.

I mentioned that a Love story generally has a happy ending. We don't have a happy ending here, we have an *everlasting marvelous beginning*. A new era starts between human beings and God, among human beings themselves — the time of *reconciliation*. At this moment, God in Jesus looks very weak and vanquished. But what we contemplate there has been powerful for generations of people in history and can be powerful for us today — because this is *the powerful weakness of Love* (1 Cor 1:25).

*Pietà**

Now we reach the end of the story. Jesus has died. His days are over, the day is over. It is getting dark, and the dead have to be buried before the Sabbath begins. So a few men and women, his disciples and his mother, take Jesus' body from the cross, anoint it with a hundred pounds of myrrh and aloes, and put it in the tomb. Christian piety has invented and inserted a special event there that is probably true. Many Christian artists have painted or sculpted the scene. They put Jesus, first of all, into the hands of his mother Mary. We have all seen what is called the Pietà.

It is good to take time and contemplate Mary holding her son in her arms. We can smell the ointments' fragrance, hear a very deep silence, see some tears. But above all, we can picture the gentleness and care of Mary and Jesus' followers, while they are anointing that beloved body, while they are touching that Love.

Ah, if only we had been there! But we have been. I suspect that many of us have experienced such a powerful moment. Do you remember when you did the same thing with your own son who was sick, with your daughter after her surgery? Do you remember what you did with your spouse or friend when he or she was slowly dying? A few weeks before I wrote this page, I was part of a Pietà in

---

*Mt 27:57–61; Mk 15:42–47; Lk 23:50–56; Jn 19:38–42.

a place of hospice care. Some friends of mine were kiss-
ing and caressing tenderly their husband and father who
was dying of cancer; I did the same with him, my friend.
I remember also the way I helped a mother put her four-
year-old daughter, Paula, who had died from a brain tumor,
into the casket. I cannot forget what I would like to have
done with my dying brother, I cannot forget what I did do
with my own dying mother.

Do we remember? Do I remember? Our hands do. Only
our fingers can relate what we said with them, what kind
of love we tried to express. That's what Mary and the
disciples did with Jesus' body, with Mary certainly remembering how she used to caress her infant's body, years
earlier in Bethlehem. God, once again like a child, was
sleeping in her hands, in our hands. Our dead child.

At that specific moment, their hands were God's hands
remembering the whole story. "Up from the bed of a
river God scooped the clay; and by the bank of the river
He kneeled Him down... this Great God, like a mammy
bending over her baby, kneeled down in the dust toiling
over a lump of clay till He shaped it in His own image,"
wrote James Weldon Johnson in the last century about
Adam's creation. Now, through a mother's tenderness,
God caresses once again this earthly body of the new Adam
who was among us the perfect image and likeness of God.
We'll never *totally* grasp God's tenderness shown here. But
we probably got something of that, because our hands were
God's love too for the ones we caressed during their difficult hours. And we remember the feeling that we could
never *totally* express our tenderness. "The hour has come,"
Jesus had said, the evening before (Jn 17:1). Mary's, the
disciples' and God's last hour had come, the hour when
their care and tenderness were for the last time God's care
and tenderness. Contrary to all the people who had disfigured that Jesus, they were the touching and caressing proof
of God's love for the Crucified One.

Three years ago, God had said to him, near the Jordan

river, "You are my Beloved Son, on whom my favor rests"
(Mk 1:11). They were God's favor resting on Jesus for the
last minutes. We can thank these men and women who
were there. They were the ones crying over God's body,
they were God crying. At the right hour, we have been, we
are sacraments of God's love and favor for a beloved son
or a daughter of God who is somehow crucified, when our
hands speak our love by their gentle and extremely delicate
touch.

If we look around ourselves, we see that it is always the
hour for us to do the same, individually and collectively,
for all the crucified ones. We can touch these disfigured
Jesus-bodies and anoint their wounds in many different
ways. Each hour is an opportunity to be God's favor resting
on crucified human beings. And let us hope that if we are
the crucified one, a merciful person will come to us with
aromatic herbs and a gentle touch. Such a behavior has a
name in the Bible: *compassion*.

Today, we are in charge of God's compassion for the
ones who hurt because of sin. And we must start with ourselves, being full of care for our body, mind, and heart, and
no longer beating them up as Balaam did with his don-
key (Nm 22:22–34). We must do this because they are our
closest companion, servant, and neighbor, and because it
is the best way to learn how to do what we are called to
do with others. God delivers all victims into our hands,
sure that we have enough myrrh and aloes, enough love
in our heart for accomplishing that mission of compassion. The proof of that possibility is already visible. For
instance, we are fortunate to have many people working
or volunteering in hospitals and psychiatric institutions,
convalescent homes, and prisons (but the needs are still
so great!). There are also the ones fighting on all levels
of society for less racism, more justice and peace (but the
struggle is not yet over). "Go, and do the same," said Jesus
to a scribe after describing what the Good Samaritan did
(Lk 10:37). God needs good Samaritans for the wounds

of ourselves and of our society. God has no other good Samaritans on earth but us.

If we have been touched by some good Samaritans in our life, we know how we felt; therefore we can anticipate the feeling of the ones we are going to anoint: a feeling of *joy*. But is that joy comparable to the joy we savored when *we* did what I have described, at the bedside of a spouse or a parent, of a child or a friend? It is a painful joy, but it is a unique joy. If we take care of all our crucified brothers and sisters, our joy will be immense, because it is God's own joy.

On Golgotha it was God's hour of compassion for all humankind through Jesus. Now it is still God's hour of compassion for all of us, but through all of us. We are the new body of Christ for people, so we are his hands and heart; so let us do what God did for us through Jesus' body. When we contemplate these men and women taking such care of the Crucified One, we cannot miss the call to take care in our turn of the crucified ones, within us and around us — as the hands of "the God of the lowly, the helper of the oppressed, the supporter of the weak, the protector of the forsaken, the savior of those without help" (Jdt 9:11).

Probably it was not easy for the disciples and Mary to handle Jesus' body. It will never be easy for us to cope with our crucified being or other crucified human beings. When it is too difficult, may we remember that we have another opportunity to see Jesus' body in our hands. It happens when we receive that special Bread at communion time, during our eucharistic services. It is not a dead body, even though it is motionless. It is, according to our faith, the Body of the Risen Jesus, who is alive forever.

When we have in our hands the body of a newborn baby, it is life that we hold, such a life that many grandparents are rejuvenated by the experience! How much more can we be rejuvenated with the Risen One at the tips of our fingers. When it is not easy for us to keep in our hands the crucified ones, let us take the Risen One, and we'll become stronger. That Bread of Life, that Bread of Love, will feed our strength and our courage. Fed by Love, we'll love more easily. Nourished by the Body of the Risen One, we'll be able to nourish the bodies of the crucified ones.

At that moment, we won't hear God asking us the question of Jesus to Peter, "Do you love me?" — because it will be obvious that we are feeding God's lambs, that we are tending God's sheep (Jn 21:15–17).

Excluded*

H E DIED. On Golgotha, just outside of Jerusalem, on "the mountain of the Lord, ... he whose hands are sinless, whose heart is clean" (Ps 24:3–4). It is helpful to trace the tragedy out on a map. Most Jews are inside the walls of the city. The Romans are behind the walls of the Antonia fortress, their residence during the Jewish holidays, which overlooks the Temple. Someplace else in the city the disciples are hiding after having "locked the doors of the place ... for fear of the Jews" (Jn 20:19). Everyone is behind walls! *Outside* of all these enclosures is Jesus. *Excluded.* Absolutely excluded in a tomb guarded by the Jewish authorities, sealed in death. Excluded from the living. "I have become an outcast to my brothers, a stranger to my mother's sons," said the psalmist (Ps 69:9).

He is excluded by the crowd, by the civil and religious lawmakers who refuse the God who was preached by this rebel and blasphemer (Acts 4:27). A God of love? As heads of institutions they prefer a God of order and discipline, no doubt. A God of the voiceless and powerless *anawim!* These people did not count in a time without elections. A God of sinners? For Jews only the just were pleasing to God; for the pagan philosophers it was only the wise. "The prostitutes will enter the kingdom before you," he had said. "Today you will be with me in paradise," he promised a thief (Mt 21:31; Lk 24:43). His adversaries refuse to

---

*Mt 21:39; Mk 12:8; Lk 20:15.

accept that, and we do the same today. He is excluded because he had become in many ways an *outlaw* according
to their norms. "The tenants seized him, dragged him outside the vineyard, and killed him," was the way he worded
one of his announcements of the Passion (Mt 22:39). As
an outlaw, he dies outside of the walls of the City and of
the Synagogue.

When we picture the Hebrews' nomadic life we realize
that to be an outlaw, rejected by one's tribe in the desert,
is to die. In our society to be an outcast means "social"
death at the least, and sometimes physical death as well.
Jesus, locked into death, is like a convict prohibited by a
restraining order from entering the space of the living, outside of the Jerusalem where live those who write, comment
on, and apply the laws. These laws, which are meant to
preserve the common good and should have acquitted him
because he was innocent, protect instead the guilty. The
walls I am talking about are the barriers that our laws,
norms, and standards can become, the ones we define and
the ones we take shelter behind. "Laws can be wal(l)s, if
we change the arrangement of the letters," someone said
to me! As the Good Shepherd, Jesus had come and wanted
to bring back the lost sheep into the sheepfold. His enemies, on the contrary, as the ninety-nine self-righteous
sheep, cast him out — both him and his message — out in
death, which was for them the final place for sinners. And
we often do the same through our laws — cast people out,
behind the walls of our norms.

I see some little children in my neighborhood already
adept at exclusion. "We don't want you to play with us!"
they say to anybody who won't go along with their rules.
Single mothers are kept apart from the family because of
the law of reputation. Homosexuals are treated as though
they have the plague and are excluded from jobs and some
social groups simply because we have defined the laws
of sexuality. The poor are wallowing in misery far from
the American Dream because it's the middle class that

makes its rules. Children of color are not welcome in
some schools and neighborhoods because our norms are
the same color as our skin. History is filled with instances
of people who are excommunicated from Churches. The
world would be different if laws were made by the people that society now excludes. We are often the ninety-nine
self-righteous sheep rejecting the others.

Behind their laws are Jesus' adversaries very alive? "He
who rejects me, rejects the One who sent me," Jesus
warned (Lk 10:16). By excluding Jesus they have rejected
God's life of Love, like the ones who wanted to stone
the adulterous woman, who was an outlaw (Lv 20:10; Dt
22:22). Invited to look at their own sins, they disappeared
from the scene: They sought to exclude and eventually excluded themselves. To exclude is to exclude oneself. Judas
betrayed and excluded his Master from his life; he excluded
himself from Jesus' friends (Jn 8:9; 13:30; Mt 26:69). So
Jesus' adversaries exclude themselves from Love and Life.
And what we see in them are precisely the symptoms of
division and death, for all of the characters of the Passion
are possessed by *fear and hatred.* Seemingly secure behind
their walls, never risking to come out, they cannot taste
what this verse wished them, "May peace be within your
walls, Jerusalem" (Ps 122:7).

Romans and Jews are divided and scared by their fear of
one another. The Romans are afraid of rebellion; the Jews
of deadly retaliation. They hate each other. The disciples
are separated from the rest of the Jews, and will be persecuted and martyred by them, starting with Stephen and
James (Acts 7; 8:1–3; 12:2). Many of the Jews hate the
Christians. They are probably afraid of their heresy. And
the disciples themselves are scared behind their "locked
doors." (A time will come when Christians will generously
reimburse the Jews with centuries of bloody persecution!)

Jerusalem on that Friday is a good image of our society. Our exclusive behavior kills love and life. When
the Sun-King rejected the Protestants, France lost a lot of

skillfulness that was forced into exile and flourished else-where. In our prisons we are perpetuating a huge waste of money and the loss of the real or potential talent that prisoners possess, because we fail to address the economic and social roots of crime in our society. The European Churches, thinking they were unifying by suppressing dif-ference, never took into consideration the culture of the people they baptized; they deprived themselves of the cul-tural richness of India, Africa, China, Japan, the Americas. This has only increased our divisions.

Our expressions "Third World" and "North-South" im-ply a world divided. Our terms "upper class," "middle class," and "lower class" repeat the same thing on a na-tional level. We hate easily: Protestants and Catholics have hated one another; some rich people hate poor people and vice versa; some whites hate blacks and vice versa. The boundary lines of different sections of the city often reflect the divisions of a society full of fear.

When I first came to the United States in 1971, I was driven through Harlem in New York City. The Sisters who were giving me a tour said, "Lock your door!" The first time I walked by myself through downtown Monrovia, Liberia, I felt so insecure, being the only white person around, that I quickly "retreated" to the place where I was giving a retreat. The one we define as the other always seems like a stranger, but Jesus said, "I was a stranger and you welcomed me" (Mt 25:35). We are far from welcoming; in fact, we often exclude the other as an outlaw.

The way of the cross is an ordinary occurrence: It is any process of exclusion. When we exclude someone, Love is making the way of the cross, suffering and sometimes dying at the end. Each time I see an elderly person aban-doned, a foreigner expelled, someone committed to an iso-lated place like a prison or a psychiatric institution, I see Love dying along the way, because of some disease in all of us. For very often these events are the symptoms of a so-cietal illness that has not been treated. In the same way

that insane people are often the signs of insane relationships in society, any outlaw is the manifestation of a social
problem that has not been solved. An outlaw is a question
that creates a crack in the walls of the laws; love must enter this open space and discover an answer. Once again I'll
quote Qohelet (probably having Moses and Jacob in mind):
"I observe that all who live under the sun side with the
child, the second one and the *usurper*" (Eccl 4:15; Ex 2; Gn
25:19–34).

Something new, a new life wants to be born in society,
through the one we put aside. But we misread the event
and give the wrong answer. Frequently it is because of poverty, lack of education, and a dysfunctional family life that
some people eventually end up on the street or in jail, as
prostitutes or criminals, as outlaws. What does our love
answer in the face of that? Here is an example from the
correctional system. An official once said, "We have built a
lot of prisons, imagining this as a solution to crime. What
if the health care system, faced with an epidemic of diar-
rhea, said 'Let us build more toilets?'" To exclude people
is to ignore the real issue and the right answer, and at
the same time to hurt and kill the life of Love in the one
thrown beyond our walls. In Jesus this became abundantly
clear.

He had spent his time, as had other prophets, trying to
cure Israel. He had pointed out the real issue, the lack of
agape. Many did not hear him. Similarly, conscientious ob-
jectors were unheard outlaws in many countries for a long
time, until some governments recognized their own duty
to respect the philosophical or religious convictions of all
individuals. Amnesty International works on behalf of outlaws, persecuted because of their political orientation; the
issue is freedom of speech. As a matter of fact, in some
places it was outlaws who were the first to denounce dictatorships. Outlaws are saying something we must hear. "He
who has ears to hear, let him hear," as Jesus also said (Mt
11:15). We must listen to outlaws and discover, beyond

their immediate words and behaviors, *what exactly* they are telling us about our society. Then, having heard them, we need to risk going outside of the (apparent) safety we savor behind our norms, behind our walls. But the Passion goes even further. A few faithful remained beside the Crucified One on Golgotha. So are we invited to stay beside all the outlaws and outcasts. They are often the crucified ones of our day. God is beside them, because the Father was beside his crucified Son. God *"hears* the cry of the poor," and its meaning (Ps 34:7). This began when God heard the cry of the outlaws and outcasts of Egyptian society, the Hebrews (Ex 2:23–24).

What a strange God! A God on the side of outlaws. The Pharisees asked the disciples, "Why does your teacher eat with tax collectors and sinners?" They were probably as surprised as we are to hear this answer: "Go and learn what this means — I desire mercy and not sacrifice" (Mt 9:11–12). In Jesus we find the same God who asks us to be merciful and compassionate toward those who are excluded. In fact, caring for them is for our own benefit.

Moreover, God is holy, *apart,* as I have said earlier. That God exists beyond the margins of everything and dares to love to the point of being rejected by us *outside* of our walls. So God must have a kind of similarity with the outcasts marginalized by the laws we write. As long as we confine ourselves to the texts we have written, we'll certainly miss something about God, about Love. The margin is the only place where something new can be written, and in the Gospels we see marginalized people proving that. In Luke, it is a marginalized woman who demonstrates a love absolutely new to Simon, the Pharisee; it is a Roman centurion, a pagan, who expressed a faith found "not even in Israel"; it is the tenth leper, a Samaritan, twice an outlaw, who wrote the word the nine other Jews had left out of their text, the word of gratitude (Lk 7:36–50; 7:1–10; 17:11–19).

God's Silence?

W HILE JESUS IS RESTING in the tomb, we enter into
God's unfathomable silence. It has been there since
the beginning of the Passion, but now it seems awfully
deep. Only Jesus' adversaries are talking. They ask Pilate
for guards around the tomb. They were noisy during the
Passion. They are still the same after it (like those people
who talk nonstop during a funeral!).

Jesus is dead, so the Word of God in our flesh is mute.
And the One he called "Abba" seems silent too. Everybody and everything is at rest. This is normal; it was a
Great Sabbath, John tells us (Jn 19:31). "For when peace-
ful stillness compassed everything, and the night in its
swift course was half spent, your all-powerful Word from
heaven's royal throne bounded, a fierce warrior, into the
doomed land," says the book of Wisdom, and the Word
became flesh among us (Wis 18:14–15; Jn 1:14). Now,
in the still night of death, the powerful warrior in our
no-longer-doomed land rests.

The disciples probably rested, as we do after the death
of someone we loved or when after a long struggle, we have
exhausted all our questioning. When we have spent our
strong emotions, we are worn out; we rest. Then the companion we need most is silence. Jesus rests too, in death.
Sent by his Father to the vineyard, he has worked very
hard. Yes, Jesus, you deserve to rest. Do it, we'll keep a
vigil beside you, as we do at the bedside of a sick child
or a dying friend. God rests too. Out of silence, God had

talked over the chaos. And when Creation was finished, on the seventh day God rested silently (Gn 1). On Golgotha *re-creation* through Jesus has been painfully done: "All is accomplished" (Jn 19:30). So respectful of that Great Sabbath, God can rest silently again.

Silently. We could stay silent for a long time before God's silence, letting it enter into us, as it did into the tomb, as it does when we let it penetrate our emptiness after any death has pierced our heart (Mt 27:57). Poor God... it had been hard too for God. For Christian faith, Jesus is the Son of God: In him God's passionate love for humankind became a *sorrowful* Passion. Through him, Christians believe in a God who *can suffer.* "What could be the use of a God unable to suffer?" asked a friend of mine. As Christians we can say that the Father *himself* suffers because the Son did, even though here we approach the ultimate paradox. God suffers silently. But this silence speaks loudly about, first of all, the immense respect God has for our freedom, a respect for the very freedom with which we killed Jesus.

God silently and painfully watched over the great Exodus of all human beings from the land of their sins, led by the new Moses, Jesus. God silently kept a painful vigil, as we do when we witness a difficult delivery. God seems silent, but "silence gives consent." According to Hebrews, Christ "when he came into the world... said — I come to do your will" (Heb 10:5–7). So God too says yes to the logic of love that wanted to save all of us, that wanted to deliver us at any price. God says yes to the way of the cross we had decided: "Let it be done according to your word" (Lk 1:37). God, in and with Jesus, says, "Wherever you go, I will go, wherever you live, I will live.... Wherever you die, I will die" (Ru 1:16–17).

We have shared that yes, each time we uttered it in the face of the departure or death of a cherished one. But when our daughter leaves for college, when our son gets married, it might be painful, but it is also a beginning. Death hurts, but if we believe, it is also the gate of a beginning. God knew that death was not the end, even though *nothingness* apparently prevailed all around to the point that we don't have one single word about what Jesus' friends did that Saturday.

With Jesus dead, everything certainly looked dead for them. When our beloved goes away or dies, everything becomes gray and colorless. When love seems gone or dead for or in us, life is tasteless and swallowed by a sort of nothingness. Nothingness. In that nothingness, the disciples were waiting, God knows where, God knows for what. When this is our situation, we feel lost, empty, and nowhere, and we wait. For what? Nothingness has nothing to offer, many people would say. But they are absolutely wrong!

At the beginning God created everything from nothingness, says Christian faith. Nothingness is therefore God's time, for only God can create, recreate from nothingness. Nothingness is a pregnancy for everything, because precisely when there is nothingness, everything is possible. "Nothing is impossible for God," was said to Mary's faith, and the One who is Everything came (Lk 1:37). Nothingness is the time of faith and hope. That Saturday, so different from all Saturdays, was holy because never did humankind know such a "hope against hope," as we knew in the face of that dead body (Rom 4:18–19). An old tradition attributes such hope, such faith to Mary, who knew since the Incarnation that God could succeed where there was nothingness. And God did more than what humanity hoped for: God woke Jesus up from the dead.

God's Passion launches a new life; all our Passions can hurl us into new life as well. "Death is swallowed up in victory. Death, where is your victory? Death, where is your sting?" exults Paul (1 Cor 15:54–55). But to fully develop this thought now would be to talk and pray about the Risen One. I want to remain with the Passion; so I'll say just this. Jesus had announced, "The third day, I will be raised to life" (Mt 16:21). God acted fast...From Friday mid-afternoon till Sunday at dawn, we have to count three days somehow! Short ones! This is no surprise: God was in a hurry to exalt Jesus, to give him back life. God is always in a hurry to bring us back to a life of love. And we are always in a hurry for the love that is born again in us for ourselves or someone else, or within others for us.

And God is still in a hurry today to give us victory over any kind of death. But God's silence, like the silence preceding the first notes of a new symphony, tells us something more about our life to come. After finishing Creation, God entrusted it to us human beings. After starting re-creation, God entrusts it to you and me. If God looks silent, it is that *we* have to talk. God's silence says that time has come for us to be God's Word — *Dabar* in Hebrew, meaning word and action. In fact, God has always talked through human mouths and hands. As the previous chapters make clear, God never stopped talking through the actors of the Passion, from Mary in Bethany to Jesus. Not always verbally, to be sure; Van Gogh's painting *Crows over a Wheat Field* says volumes about his insanity; Michelangelo's sculpture *The Pietà* speaks eloquently about sorrow; the Icon of the Crucified says a lot about Love, silently. Now God wants to talk and act through you and me according to Jesus' way, and already does.

One of the best examples for me is what is going on concerning AIDS. Indeed, in the sufferings and the body of the sick we can hear the Crucified One. But here I am thinking more of the other side of the picture. Thousands of men and women are working in laboratories all over the world to overcome the plague of our century. A lot of people donate money and time to support this undertaking. Many politicians are fighting for the policies still needed to promote the welfare of the ones who suffer from the disease. A multitude of individuals and groups pray for the patients, their families and friends. Is that not a fantastic word and action of care and compassion from God?

God silent? We hear there a beautiful symphony of concern and dedication, of love. A far cry from some deadly words expressed at the beginning.

God silent? God probably never talks as loudly as in a Passion. God-Justice rebelled against my mother's death, saying, "She did not get the right treatment because of her poverty!" God-Peace sadly asked me through the last soldier of my regiment killed, in 1957, in the war between France and Algeria, "Why are people killing each other for nothing?" God-Life spoke to me through seven dead people on a French highway, "Why are some drivers speeding unreasonably under the influence of alcohol or drugs?" God-Reconciliation laments before me each time I see pictures of the Middle East, South Africa, former Yugoslavia, or Northern Ireland, "How can you accept all those deaths created by racism, misuse of religion, and other so-called reasons?" God-Bread weeps in front of me when thousands of children die of starvation in Somalia or suffer from malnutrition in the United States, and implores, "Why do you destroy your own flesh and blood, my little ones?"

When we face the body of the Crucified One, the bodies of all crucified ones, I hope that questions arise within us. God has the same questions. If we are not deaf, we hear not God's silence but God's sorrow. Death is always a question, but some deaths become God's questions about our way of governing our lives, and a call to change it. And what we call God's silence is rather God's humble prayer, "Please, take care of the world I have given to you, of the ones I have given into your hands as your brothers and sisters. And you *can* do it, because my own Spirit of Love, the Spirit of Jesus is all yours. You *can* do it, because such loving power overcomes anything that is deadly."

We must remember Ezekiel's vision. When Jerusalem and the Temple were destroyed, most of the Jews were deported. That started what is called the Diaspora, the scattering of Israel and their faith outside of Palestine. Where then was God's Presence? Ezekiel saw God's Glory — and so God's Presence and Word — leave the Temple going East, the direction of Exile. Some scholars say that Ezekiel understood that God's Presence would be henceforth in the midst of the Chosen People and no longer in the building of the Temple. God's destiny was in the Jews' hands, wherever they would be (Ez 10:18–22; 11:22–25). It is not by chance that later on God's Word appeared in Alexandria, Egypt, as the Bible written in Greek, the universal language of that time. When the Body, the Temple of God's Word, is destroyed on Golgotha, the Word of that Presence becomes *our own* where we are, in our family and neighborhood, job and city, nation and world. God has no longer one mouth and two hands only on earth, the ones of Jesus. God has now the mouth and the hands of all the people of good will. The Emmanuel, God-with-us, being dead, the new era of God-in-us starts. God is far from silent because God's Word and Action are now scattered wherever we are.

If we remember what we have heard through God's silence in the Passion, in all our individual and collective Passions, something will change. A Jewish scholar said, "The Messiah's keys are in the potter's hands." The extraordinary resides in the works we accomplish for peace, justice, and joy, day by day in our ordinary life. If we let the Spirit of God talk and work through us now, we accomplish Zechariah's prophecy: "Old men and old women will again sit down in the squares of Jerusalem.... And the squares of the city will be full of boys and girls playing there" (Zec 8:4–5). Our world will be less and less a place of destructive confrontations like a perpetual Golgotha. Our plazas will be full of new life. We will see Grandpa smoking his pipe, Grandma knitting a sweater, while watching their grandchildren leap and play without fear — for the plagues of our time will be gone.

God's Revenge

I WROTE AT THE BEGINNING of this book that if the disciples were surprised by Jesus' words and actions, it was because Jesus brought the revelation of a "new" God. Therefore I said, "By pondering these pages and using them as a help for prayer, Christians will be able to see through Jesus the beauty of their God revealed in an extraordinary way in the Passion." This beauty shines particularly through God's retaliation, announced in Isaiah 61:2, and by Jesus himself in Luke 4:16–21. For after the murder of his innocent Son, what can we expect the Father's revenge to be? Something like the day of the Lord in Joel 2, Nahum 1, or Zephaniah 1?

The guard around the tomb wants to keep everything frozen in death. But God-Love will not put up with being imprisoned and raises Jesus up, thus getting revenge on death. Passing through walls and doors, the Risen One comes back to his disciples and eventually to the Jews and the pagans. This is the moment of revenge against all those who abandoned him or killed him.

Before the Passion Jesus had his opponents describe what God's reaction would be. He had asked his adversaries, "What do you suppose the owner of the vineyard will do to those tenants [who killed his son] when he comes?" They replied, "He will bring that wicked crowd to a bad end." In another text, he himself said, "At this the king grew furious and sent his army to destroy those murderers [of his messengers] and burn their city" (Mt 21:41; 22:7). These words, which were no doubt written after the destruction of Jerusalem, are certainly based on the words of Jesus who must have described the unfortunate fate of his enemies because Luke and Mark say the same thing.

These harsh words of Jesus express an attitude appropriately biblical. "You wrong me; I avenge myself," God seems to say in the Old Testament, when the people, the leaders, or the nations are punished by events in history. Many texts depict an Israel severely punished after the adoration of the golden calf or its rebellions in the desert. And this punishment goes as far as the complete ruination of the kingdoms of Samaria and Judah. Leviticus furnishes also many other examples of the death penalty decreed for individual transgressions. The leaders? Moses, Aaron, the priests, the false prophets are punished. The kings? Since Saul, most of them were chastised because each of them "did evil in the sight of the Lord," as one refrain repeats. Two statements summarize God's revenge. "If, with all this, you still refuse to be chastened by me and continue to defy me, I, too, will defy you and will smite you for your sins seven times harder than before," and, again, in the eighth century B.C.E., "Just as the Lord took delight in making you grow and prosper, so will he now take delight in ruining and destroying you" (Lv 26:23–24; Dt 28:58–68). As for the nations, it was just as much of a catastrophe. We have only to read about the ten plagues of Egypt, the list of the kings conquered by Joshua or defeated in the wars of David, and the oracles of the prophets against the Gentiles to be convinced of this (Ex 7–12; Jos 12; 2 Sm 8). "Amorites, Hittites, Perizzites, Canaanites, Hivites and Jebusites...I will wipe them out," says God, and it was done, just like for so many others, women and children included (Ex 23:23). Will God's wrath be any less after the death of Jesus on the cross?

But it would be inadequate to stop here. Many texts proclaim another response on God's part if people have

a change of heart (like David, or Nineveh, for example)
(2 Sm 12:13; Jon 3–4). A subtle change is taking place. After the return from the Exile, a proof that God refuses to
exterminate Israel, the vengeance of God is often turned
against the nations — those who seduce the Chosen People and tempt them to sin. Israel is still punished, but the
new reasoning seems to be, "They have become an occa-
sion of sin for you; I will take revenge on *them.*" We read
in Isaiah:

> He put vengeance on like a tunic.... To each he will
> pay his due, wrath to his enemies, reprisals on his
> foes.... But for Zion, he will come as Redeemer. (Is
> 59:17–20)

What's happening is that the image that the Jews have
of God is slowly being purified. Exodus says:

> The Lord, the Lord, a merciful and gracious God, slow
> to anger and rich in kindness and fidelity, continuing
> his kindness for a thousand generations, and forgiv-
> ing wickedness and crime and sin; *yet,* not declaring
> the guilty guiltless, *but* punishing children and grand-
> children to the third and fourth generation for their
> fathers' wickedness!" (Ex 34:6–7)

Later, Deuteronomy corrects this concept:

> The Lord, your God, is God indeed, the faithful God
> who keeps his merciful covenant down to the thou-
> sandth generation toward those who love him and
> keep his commandments, *but* who repays with de-
> struction the person who hates him; he does not dally
> with such a one, but makes him personally pay for it.
> (Dt 7:9–10)

Toward 400 B.C.E., we begin to find several instances of the
following perception:

> Merciful and gracious is the Lord, slow to anger and
> abounding in kindness. He will not always chide, nor

does he keep his wrath for ever. Not according to our
sins does he deal with us, nor does he requite us according to our crimes. (Ps 103:8–10; 86:5, 15–16; Jl
2:13; Jon 4:2)

Finally, toward 300 B.C.E., Ezra prays:

But you are a God of pardons, gracious and compassionate, slow to anger and rich in mercy; you did not
forsake them. (Neh 9:17)

Progressively the words describing God as hard disappear.

What began to emerge in the Old Testament and bursts
forth in all its surprising splendor in Jesus Christ, and
above all in the Passion and the events that followed upon
it, is something new. Yes, it is "the day of vindication of
the Lord," but through forgiveness (Is 61:2). *God's revenge
is forgiveness, and forgiveness only.*

According to the scholars, the fact that God gives Jesus
back to the disciples *is* their forgiveness. Never in all of
the texts do the disciples say to the Risen One, "I am so
sorry about what I did." In the same way, Jesus never says,
"I forgive you." Why should we be surprised? He foretold
this: The prodigal father does not hear the confession of
his returning son; he does not talk about forgiveness but
only about feasting and joy because of the son he has found
again. This is similar to the two preceding parables where
the focus is also on *joy* — the joy of the shepherd who finds
his lost sheep and the joy of the woman who finds the lost
coin (Lk 15).

As for the other Jews, beginning with Acts 3, Peter
makes excuses for them, "Yet I know, brothers, that you
acted out of *ignorance*, just as your leaders did." These
words echo the voice of Jesus, "Father, forgive them; they
do not know what they are doing" (Acts 3:17; Lk 23:34).
Paul eventually would say, "I thank Christ...I received
mercy because I had acted ignorantly in unbelief" (1 Tm
1:12–13). As for the pagans, what did they know about the

God of Israel? Nothing. And so Peter says to them, "As obedient sons, do not yield to the desires that once shaped you in your ignorance" (1 Pt 1:14). What kind of ignorance are we talking about? The disciples, the adversaries knew well *what* they were doing to Jesus during the Passion. But they had no idea about *the unique nature* of the God they were crucifying in him — just as we who only scratch the surface of the being of God with our words, as apophatic theology and the mystics have always said. We ourselves know that our love for those we cherish is deeper than any description. How much more is the Love that is God far beyond our definitions and images.

Moses intercedes for his own idolatrous people:

> O Lord, why does your wrath burn hot against your people...? Why should the Egyptians say, "With evil intent did their god bring them forth, to slay them in the mountains, and to consume them from the face of the earth?" Turn from your fierce wrath, and repent of this evil against your people.... And the Lord repented of the evil which the Lord thought to do to the chosen people. (Ex 32:7–14)

This eloquent and smart plea uses an argument that we all are familiar with, "What will people think?" If God had been tempted to explode in anger on Golgotha, Jesus would have spoken just like Moses. If they saw God's rage, people would have said, "Hey, this God is just like the gods we have always known who, in our own image and likeness, punish people and get revenge when they are offended!" Maybe Jesus' prayer, "Father, forgive them, they do not know what they are doing," expressed his last temptation and his last victory (Lk 23:34). Perhaps, at the last minute, Jesus was afraid that God would retaliate as usual! So he interceded for us, and won, for God did not smash his enemies. He could do so, for he knew that God had already started to soften in Hosea, "I will not give vent to my blazing anger...For I am God and not man. I will not let the flames consume you" (Hos 11:9).

But the Passion shows that God does not forgive as we usually do. We tend to see *first* the offense committed *against us* or the pain that it has caused *us*. *Then* we appeal to our love to make the best of the offense and the pain. In forgiving, afterwards, we start all over with a new relationship with the one who has hurt us. Love given back, like the Risen One was to his disciples, is what forgiveness means. But God does not act this way exactly, according to Jesus' words. The father had divided up the property and given his younger son the share of the estate that was coming to him. This was already a beautiful gift. But when the son comes back, the father gives his patient waiting, his all-night vigil, his feelings, his rushing out of the house, his arms, his kisses, the finest robe, a ring, shoes, the fatted calf and a party! It's an extravaganza!

The son is guilty and yet it's the offended father who gives the most. This is what God's forgiveness is like. This is the God who, in our ignorance, we do not understand because God does not come from the offense but rather from love. Our faults call God's love *first* and foremost. Peter is using our logic when he asks, "Lord, when my brother wrongs me, how often must I forgive him, seven times?" Here he is coming from the offense and from his own sense of being the offended party. Jesus' answer was, "[Do even more than that,] seventy times seven times" (Mt 18:21–22). In a complete reversal of the verse of Deuteronomy cited above, Jesus appeals to love and challenges it seventy times "seven times harder than before" (28:58–68). The salvation that is granted to humanity in the Crucified lies in this turnabout. It's not Love just given back, because it was never withdrawn; *it's a multiplication of Love.*

The word "forgiveness" comes from the Anglo-Saxon *Giefan* or *Gifan* and *For,* and means "to give away." What is implied is a waste, an extravagance. Like Mary in Bethany, or the sower, or like the prodigal father, God sows love "bountifully" and not "sparingly," above all in forgiveness, to the point of the total gift of the Son (Jn 12:1–11; Mk 4:1–9; 2 Cor 9:6). Nehemiah 9 had already said that to each of Israel's sins corresponded a new gift from God. But Jesus took up that theme in even a stronger way. The parable about the tenant farmers of the vineyard shows a God who reasons in this way: "I have sent many messengers as my prophets. But the evidence is clear: my people have not stopped sinning, have not yet understood who I am. I must do even more. I will send my own son" (Mt 21:33–46). This God no longer says, "You've wronged me. So I will avenge myself on you or the nations." God in the extravagance of the gift of the Son affirms, "You have offended me, but it must be that I haven't done *everything* I could." I have known parents who have said the same thing without any guilt complex but out of an abundance of love, giving themselves away, in the face of serious wrongs committed by their children. And every society that is so easily tempted to get rid of its "criminal elements" by capital punishment would do well to at least ask itself this question, "In the face of such a crime, have we done enough for those who have become the guilty ones? Haven't we let the conditions that led them to their crimes develop?"

The sending of the Son, to his total gift on the cross, is the ultimate gift and so includes everything. "Love covers a multitude of sins," says Peter (1 Pt 4:8). This is our love when we are ready for *everything*, rejection and forgiveness included, and the price *we* will pay. A woman and a man who truly love and who decide to conceive or adopt a child are aware of this, if they really know what they are doing. For God, this was perfectly accomplished in the Passion, as the chorus sorrowfully sings in Handel's *Messiah*, "And the Lord hath laid on him the iniquity of us all" (Is 53:6; Mt 8:17). "Whoever has seen me, has seen the Father," Jesus said. On Calvary both took upon themselves the iniquity of us all (Jn 14:9). What an extravagance! And Jesus invites Peter, each of us, to forgive as God does.

This appeal honors us and pushes us further than we go spontaneously. When an offense is committed against me, if there is "one more mile" to go, it is *for me, the victim* (Mt 6:41). The unheard of extravagance of Love is suggested to me. Though I may suffer a sorrowful passion, I am invited to live out the passionate love of God itself. Of course, some people will say that to accept such a crucifixion is crazy. Yes, this is what Paul talked about. As a persecutor who was the beneficiary of this foolishness of God, he could speak as an expert, "We preach Christ crucified — stumbling block to Jews, and an absurdity to Gentiles.... For God's folly is wiser than people, and his weakness more powerful than them" (1 Cor 1:18–25). God does not take delight in ruining and destroying as we do when we take revenge (Dt 28:58–68). Before our offenses, God's reaction is, *"No doubt, I haven't yet done enough for you."* And God finds delight in loving... still more, even to Golgotha. And God asks us to do the same thing, because that is the way God "judges the world with justice and the peoples with equity" (Ps 98:9).

No one ever said it would be easy. What can help us to forgive is to become aware before the Crucified of all that God has given and forgiven us. We are all like the insolvent official "who owed his king a huge amount" and saw his debt written off. How could we not write off the debt of the ones who owe us "a mere fraction" of what we ourselves owe (Mt 18:21–35; Lk 7:42)? When we must forgive and if we are "weary and find life burdensome," let's call upon the Love that dwells in us, the Love of God itself (Rom 5:5). Then we will experience the truth of Jesus' words, "Your souls will find rest, for my yoke is easy and my burden light" (Mt 11:29–30).

But why is God doing that, and therefore has the right to ask us to do likewise? Through Ezekiel God said, "And you shall know that I am the Lord when I deal with you thus, *for my name's sake*, and not according to your evil conducts and corrupt actions, O House of Israel" (Ez 20:44). And through Isaiah, "For the sake of my name I restrain my anger, for the sake of my renown I hold it back from you, lest I should destroy you" (Is 48:9). Jeremiah prayed, "We recognize that we have sinned against you. For your name's sake spurn us not, disgrace not the throne of your glory: remember your covenant with us, and break it not" (Jer 14:21). And the Psalms take up the same theme, "Deliver us and pardon our sins for your name's sake," "For your name's sake, O Lord, you will pardon my guilt, great as it is" (Ps 79:9; 25:11). For the sake of which Name? No longer the name of the "God of vengeance" (Ps 94:1). So a "new name" (Rv 2:17)?

In the name of Jesus, no doubt, through whom salvation has been given us, according to Paul. "Jesus who "is Lord, to the glory of God the Father" (Phil 2:9–11). But also the name of the One we know better now, through the Passion. Who? Love, Father, Compassion, Mercy, Gift, Forgiveness, Nourishment, Reconciliation, Vulnerability, Extravagance, Other, Holy? All these names represent admirable qualities of God, but they do not adequately express the God perceived in the Passion. For Jesus crucified fully reveals the God who was predicted in the Old Testament, a God who is beyond all our utterances. And particularly in the act of forgiveness. It may be a good idea in this instance to follow our Jewish brothers and sisters. For ages they have not dared to pronounce God's name. This name, which no longer is uttered, was said when Moses learned, through the burning bush, for the first time God's compassion toward us (Ex 3). Perhaps we can imitate their behavior at times, not so much out of what we call "respect," but simply because no word — even the word "God" — can totally express the One who is present in the forgiveness of the Crucified-Risen One, this burning Love we can always call "You":

You, who "remembered [your] kindness and faithfulness." (Ps 98:3)

You, who are patient and kind. You, who are not jealous and who don't put on airs. You who are not snobbish. You who are never rude, never self-seeking, never prone to anger, and never brood over injuries. You who never rejoice in what is wrong but rejoice with the truth. There is no limit to your forbearance, to your trust, your hope, your power to endure. You, who never fail. (1 Cor 13)

It Is Written[*]

CONCERNING HIS PASSION, Jesus often quotes Scripture. He talks about what is happening or is going to happen, "so that the Scriptures may be fulfilled." That antiphon is not the magical sensing of some fated future. Our experience shows that in certain cases what is going to happen is written, as it were. A couple is torn apart, we foresee a divorce. An economic crisis hits our country, we anticipate strikes. In Haiti, President Aristide must have foreseen his 1991 overthrow, because the army, the rich, and the Church hierarchy opposed him more and more. The analysis of a situation permits us to predict the future. Jesus was as smart as anybody else. As soon as he realized that the powerful in Israel were "prowling around like a roaring lion, looking for someone to eat," he knew that misfortune would strike him. Thomas even said, when Jesus decided to go to Lazarus' tomb, "Let us also go to die with him" (1 Pt 5:8; Jn 11:16). Besides, Jesus had only to read Israel's history in order to discover what awaited him, because *it was written.*

He tells his adversaries the parable of the tenant farmers of the vineyard. They "realized he was speaking about them," and he says to their face, "Thus you show that you are the sons of the prophets' murderers. Now it is your turn: fill up the vessel measured out by your forefathers

---

*Mt 26:24, 31, 54, 56; Mk 9:12; 14:21, 27, 49; 15:28; Lk 18:31; 22:37; 24:44, 46; Jn 13:18; 15:25; 17:12; 19:24, 28, 36, 37.

... until retribution overtakes you for all the blood of the just ones, shed on earth, from the blood of holy Abel to the blood of Zechariah son of Barachiah, whom you murdered between the temple building and the altar.... O Jerusalem, Jerusalem, murderess of prophets and stoner of those who were sent to you" (Mt 21:33–46; 23:37–39). He refers to some traditions that tell him what he can expect. He certainly prayed with the litany of the sins of Israel in Scripture (Neh 9; Bar 1–3). "Well aware of what was in one's heart," he knew that his people would fall into the same errors over and over again and that the powerless and the prophets would pay the price (Jn 2:25). A lowly man, alone and powerless, a rejected prophet, Jesus was able to foretell his Passion. The Baptist's assassination let him preserve no illusions. So there was nothing magic about any of it: He would pay the price of his own free choice. It was written in the repeated refusals of Israel.

A Sinful and Holy History

We are like those Jews. In our own history, we see the same demons always at work. It is written. Only a few decades after Hitler, neo-Nazis sow the seeds of violence in many a democracy. After having been liberated from colonialism, people tear each other apart all over the world. "Bloodshed after bloodshed" (Hos 4:2). Since Cain and Abel, in the destruction of Jerusalem and Massadah, right up to the mass graves at Katyn (Poland), My Lai (Vietnam), and El Salvador, in the stories of Antigone or Socrates, in the medical reports from the concentration camps, in the memories and the wounds of the survivors, the sinful history of humanity is written. A brother kills his brother, especially if he is powerless or a prophet. This continual assassination is the sorrowful passion of human history that we choose to write. Written before Jesus, it will still be written after him. So then what did Jesus' Passion write that made any difference to the human adventure?

This question also brings back into view, in the face of all human defeats, the holy history of humanity. Sirach wrote his version concerning Israel (Sir 44–50). The author of Hebrews did as well, and he concludes with these lines, "Others were tortured.... Still others endured mockery, scourging.... they were stoned, sawed in two, put to death at sword's point; they went... needy, afflicted, tormented" (Heb 11). Non-Christian traditions also keep, in their memory or texts, the written names of innumerable witnesses. Legions of men and women, famous or not, have written an encyclopedia of service. The story of passionate love is being written even now by people who love, sometimes enough to die. History saw, before Jesus and apart from him, a crowd of saints and martyrs. So what is written, through Jesus' Passion, that is new?

When we read the Passion closely, we begin to feel that something is going on behind the scene because the text gives us a lot of hints. The angel who consoles Jesus during his agony, the fact that none of the disciples is arrested, the repentance of Peter, the return of Judas, who confesses his sin and gives the money back, the intervention of Pilate's wife, the hesitation of the procurator in condemning Jesus, the liberation of Barabbas, the assistance of Simon of Cyrene, the tears of the mourners, the act of faith of the "good" thief and of the centurion, the courageous intercession of Joseph of Arimathea with Pilate to obtain Jesus' body, the care of the faithful present at the foot of the cross and at the burial... these events are like the grace of God's victory trying in a thousand ways to forge a path through a horrible wasteland. It is almost God saying, "See, I am doing something new! Now it springs forth, do you not perceive it?" (Is 43:19). So what is new?

The Grace Written Every Day in History

When Jesus talks about his Passion, he often adds, "and on the third day [I] will rise again," echoing Hosea who wrote, "[The Lord] will revive us after two days; on the third day he will raise us up" (Mt 16:21; 17:22–23; 20:19; Hos 6:1–2). These words may well have been written by the first Christian communities, but Jesus could have said this himself, because he believed in the resurrection (Mt 22:23–33). In the Old Testament, the mention of the "third day" is frequent and laden with meaning. It's a period of time, synonymous with a journey, a "passover" in which the fate of a chosen one is involved. The outcome illustrates a victory of God in the salvation of the covenant. Once Jesus uses one of the strongest images in Scripture: "Just as Jonah spent three days and three nights in the belly of the whale, so will the Son of Man spend three days and three nights in the bowels of the earth" (Mt 12:40). He created another powerful image that was used against him by his adversaries during the Passion: "Destroy this temple and in three days I will raise it up" (Jn 2:20; Mt 26:61; 27:40, 63; Mk 14:58; 15:29).

And his resurrection wrote into history the reversal that the New Testament often describes in terms of victory (for it comes at the end of a combat — *agonia*, in the Greek of the New Testament; Rom 8:37; 1 Cor 15:55, 57; Rv 3:21). "The stone which the builders rejected has become the keystone of the structure," for the evil that seemed to have conquered was "smashed to pieces" (Mt 21:42; Mk 12:10; Lk 20:17; Is 28:16). "The Lord said to my lord: Sit at my right hand while I make your enemies your footstool," he had said himself (Lk 20:41–44; Ps 110). Yes, he the lowly one, he the prophet had conquered sin and death, like a new David against Goliath or a new Judith against Holofernes (1 Sm 17; Jdt 13; Ps 113:7–8). The Christian faith professes *the victory of God in Jesus*, because things are turned around, evil is overcome. "Grace super-

abounded," and we have all received "grace after grace" —
with all that these words say about pure gift and forgiveness (Jn 1:16; Rom 5:20; 2 Cor 4:15). Since one Friday on
Golgotha and the dawn of the following Sunday, henceforth it is written forever. But what does this victory of
Jesus change for us today, and first of all for those of us
who are still victims. What has the Passion written for all
human beings? What grace?

"Blessed Are You..."

Jesus already said something about this in the Beatitudes
(Mt 5; Lk 6). Each Beatitude consists of two clauses: The
first clause always talks about a set of circumstances that
is unfortunate; the second clause expresses a turnabout.
For the poor, the grace of God's reign; for the afflicted, consolation; for the hungry, abundance; for those who are persecuted, a reward; and for those who weep, laughter. Thus,
to those with whom he will later share their Passion, Jesus
promises the fruit of victory over evil. The Resurrection
renders justice to the Crucified One he was and, in him,
fills with grace all those who are crucified. "After death! Il-
lusory consolation!" some would snigger, remembering the
nineteenth-century sermons recommending that the poor
resign themselves to their fate here below — because they
would triumph over it in heaven! But these sermons were
based on an incomplete understanding of the texts they
used.

When Jesus says, "Blest are you poor; the reign of God
is yours," it's not because poverty is blessed but because
he is, himself, a blessing (Lk 6:20). In Scripture, the reign
he is talking about is the one established by a king according to God's heart: a liberator of his people, against
external enemies, of course, but also by justice toward the
lowly within the kingdom (Ps 72; 146). Jesus is this king
because he fights against the "enemy" and does all he can

in word and action to render justice to the poor in giving them priority, every day wherever he is (Mt 13:39; 11:2–6; Lk 4; Is 61:1–6). Since he inaugurates the grace of the reign of God, he *can* tell the poor about their good fortune: "Blest are you poor, the reign of God is yours... *because I am here, establishing it*" (and this is the same for the afflicted, the hungry, the persecuted, and those who weep). He promises a reversal of the situation for the poor because he establishes it by overpowering evil and, in his Passion, by conquering sin. And finally, this will occur in the future, *because he confides this reversal to us* when he gives us his Spirit, "makes [us] live by [his] statutes and observe [his] decrees," and sends us to act like him in the world (Ez 36:27).

We Christians make real the grace of the Beatitudes by working for the coming of the reign of God-Love. Jesus' victory over evil is still the lot of the poor today if they can say, when they see *us*, "Blessed are we, because you are here — fighting for justice and consoling the afflicted, feeding the hungry, defending those who are persecuted, bringing joy to those who weep." When we accomplish Jesus' mission, with all those who act beside us without knowing him, we write one more page of the holy history, our own page of a fantastic victory — *that of Love over sin.* So all those who suffer can say, "In oppression or sadness, in destitution or loneliness, in any kind of ordeal, love has been with us and for us through our brothers' and sisters' deeds. What a grace!" For a Christian, each time that somewhere in the world someone is acting in favor of the crucified ones and also trying "to open the eyes that are blind," it's the victory of God-Love in Jesus written again (Is 42:7). Written today.

For Christian faith, someone finally made a radical breakthrough in history and, out of the chaos of our behavior, created everything anew: Jesus. A human being, he loved to the point of suffering and dying, but perfectly, *divinely*, because it was the *very God* who loved in him, the Son. Because of who he is, his victory is *total*, all throughout the Passion.

God had prefigured such a daily victory in the holy history of the witnesses of love before Jesus; in the ones who came after him, God has written this grace every day again and again. Each one of them has known the experience of Paul: "in my own flesh I fill up what is lacking in the sufferings of Christ" (Col 1:24). And God continually writes salvation through the ones who "rescue the poor who cries out for help, the orphans, and the unassisted... [who] make joyful the heart of the widow... [who are] the eyes of the blind, and the feet of the lame, the father of the needy," who serve their neighbor to the end (Jb 29:12–16). As long as there has been and will be one human being loving like this, Jesus' total victory has been and will be won. Here is one answer to the questions asked above. The Christian faith in Jesus' Passion says something new: Now we know — if we believe — that *Love wins*. It might take time, "three" painful days, but all along the way Love triumphs. In all our struggles, we have the certainty of a victory, and we can "approach the throne of grace to receive mercy and favor and to find help in time of need" (Heb 4:16).

When hurricane Andrew hit Florida in 1992, it was a catastrophe. But every minute saw marvelous examples of people helping each other.

I remember one of my men risking his life while we were under heavy fire, to rescue another one, who he thought had been wounded, during the war between France and Algeria.

Monique is severely handicapped. But between herself and her mother, everybody can see daily an astonishing love.

Joan said, "I hated and loved the time when my father was dying. I hated it because he was suffering and dying, and so was I in my own way. But I loved it because we had never expressed so freely to each other so much love."

In December 1992, in Northern California, a couple and their baby were caught in a severe snowstorm and got stuck in their snowbound truck with a few crackers and a piece of cake. After five nights they decided to do something. They walked twelve miles through drifts up to waist-high until they found shelter under a ledge. The mother stayed there with the baby, nursing him and melting ice in his mouth for water. The father walked twenty-two more hours until he found help. Hours later, the three of them were safe in a hospital. The parents were treated for severe frostbite to their toes and feet and for hypothermia. After eight full days in the wilderness, the baby boy, five months old, was unharmed.*

I could pile up the examples. In a situation that is full of sufferings, that is not *yet* a medical or social, economic or political victory, Love has been there. Therefore, even though the hurt of the ordeal might focus our attention on what is still bad, it is obviously visible that *Love, as such, has already won.* Like the disciples we can say, "Lord, even the demons were subject to us because of your name." And we can hear Jesus replying, "I have observed Satan fall like lightning from the sky. Behold, I have given you the power 'to tread upon serpents' and scorpions and upon the full force of the enemy and nothing will harm you" (Lk 10:17–19). And each time this victory is written among us in our present moment, we are *all* blessed, either as the ones serving others or as the ones who have been taken care of.

So we see through Jesus' Passion that the two human histories — sinful and holy, of forgiveness and inspiration — actually write one single story: the history of the

---

*Hartford Courant, January 8, 1993.

all-powerful grace of God that always blows up sin. The victorious Passion of God makes itself visible through our Passion, which is the endless repetition in each of us of what was perfectly accomplished in Jesus of Nazareth on Golgotha, "once for all" (Rom 6:10; Heb 7:27; 9:12, 26; 10:10).

"Emmanuel," God-with-us, and Even More

Pantheists accept a certain presence of God everywhere, but it is usually somewhat vague in a historical sense. On the contrary, for Christians, God was *historically* seen in Jesus, in whom "the fullness of deity resided in bodily form" (Col 2:9). John's words tell us that we have seen and heard, contemplated and touched the Word of Life "that was present to the Father and became visible to us" in the man of Nazareth (1 Jn 1:1–2). In Jesus, God was directly and personally, historically, the object of the human Passion. It is written *in* our history, because it was written *in* the blood and flesh of a human being, Jesus. But this historicity of God's Presence continues. God is no longer just *with* us, but *in* us. It is no longer the god of mythologies who visited us, and then went back home. Tourist, voyeur, or merciful one, this god never fully shared our condition, and above all never our sufferings. It is no longer the God of the Old Testament who acted through somebody else, angel or prophet. If we believe that Jesus is the Son of the God he called "Father," if we believe that he has given us their own Spirit, we believe that God not only "made his dwelling among us," but *is now in* us (Jn 1:14). Therefore, we can no longer be alone.

While I am writing these lines, several places in Bosnia-Herzegovina are besieged and shelled. In these furnaces where we may be, Someone is there. It is no longer God's angel, just beside us, the Shadrach, Meschach, and Abed-

nego of today, according to Daniel; it is God there *in* us
(Dn 3).

If someone is in a concentration camp, the love of and
for a spouse, a child, a friend does not change anything and
changes everything. Nothing is changed, for the violence of
torture remains torture. However, it would be only where
suffering exists without love that there could be written the
word "Hell." On the contrary, the presence of love writes
a change in the midst of fire or raging waters. God did
not promise that the waves will subside or the flames die
down, but says, "Fear not...I will be with you," but guaranteed, "In the rivers you shall not drown, when you walk
through fire, you shall not be burned" (Is 43:1–5). In the
worst ordeals, the ones who love and are loved cannot be
annihilated; they are victorious because love gives them an
unbelievable strength. Love keeps them "on [their] feet" (Ez
2:2). This has been written in thousands of people who
experienced that. Paul said, about himself and other ministers of the Good News, "We are afflicted in every way, but
not constrained; perplexed but not driven to despair; persecuted but not abandoned; struck down but not destroyed."
His explanation is, "I live by faith in the Son of God who
has loved me and given himself up for me" (2 Cor 4:8–9;
Gal 2:20). To all, starting with Jesus in his Passion, Paul's
words can be applied:

> We even boast of our afflictions, knowing that af-
> fliction produces endurance, and endurance, proven
> character, and proven character, hope, and hope does
> not disappoint, because the love of God has been
> poured out into our hearts through the holy Spirit
> that has been given us. (Rom 5:3–5)

Love has been the strength and victory of all martyrs.
This is also written for us who undergo more common-
place sufferings. We are no longer alone, for we are loved
and inhabited by Someone who is totally imbedded within
us in all our passions. Paul's word is true for *everybody*

who suffers, believer or nonbeliever: "Neither death, nor life, nor angels, nor principalities, nor present things, nor future things, nor powers, nor height, nor depth, nor any other creature will be able to separate us from the love of God in Christ Jesus our Lord" (Rom 8:38–39). When asking for our help, God did not say, "Change the heart of the Jewish leaders, of Pilate, or of the crowd." In Jesus, God only begged, "Keep watch with me" (Mt 26:38). God knows that the worst part of any terrible trial is when love is not there.

If God is in us through Jesus' Spirit, God has no other body, no other heart than ours, according to Paul (1 Cor 12). Therefore, something new is written in all our sorrowful or loving passions. Every human being is henceforth *a sacrament* of God's grace. What was only a hope has become a comfort because, in faith, it is a certainty. Since Jesus we delight in more than just Emmanuel — "God-*with*-us"; we enjoy God-*in*-us, because we are Jesuslike, Christlike (Mt 1:23). It's no longer just God-as-food when we receive the Bread and the Wine; not just God-as-Word when we hear or read the Scriptures; not just God-as-balm each time we are anointed; it's God as human flesh and blood.

The sacramentality of God's presence and victory through our brother or sister reveals a God who is no longer present in a mythical way. God suffers and loves *in* us. God aches *in* the one who undergoes an ordeal because of our sin. Jesus himself guaranteed it, when he said to the ones who care for suffering people, "What you did for one of these least ones, you did it for *me*" (Mt 25:40, 45). And that climaxed in the Crucified Jesus on Golgotha. But God suffers also *in* any torturer, as wounded Love, as Love trying desperately to survive, as God-Tears but God-Hope.

On the other hand, it *is* God-Courage in us when we give up being wolves, cowards, or sluggards, and serve. It's God-Care who *is* the gentleness of a mother's eyes or the warmth of a father's voice, the sad little smile of our child or the care of the nurse when we are sick. It's God-Tenderness who *is* our caress as a spouse or as a friend when we are at the bedside of our dying partner. It's God-Service who *is* the obliging taxi driver or gas station attendant when we are lost. It's God-Competence who *is* the earnestness of a boss or a co-worker when our company is in crisis. It's God-Boldness who *is* the courage of the honest politician or religious leader confronting an injustice. It's Jesus' God-Everywhere, it's Jesus' *God-Here*, each time we abandon our being and our doing to this grace of the Crucified-Risen One *in* us, the Spirit of Love. This is written forever.

In the sacrament of our brother or sister, we see a God who acts justly, loves mercy, and walks humbly with us (Mi 6:8). It is not the triumphant God of Sinai or of the vision of Isaiah; it is a God extremely close to us, suffering, but also saving *there in* the simple presence of a man or a woman, of you and me every day (Ex 19:16–19; Is 6:1–4). God was seen accomplishing salvation in Jesus, and God has not stopped being visible as such a Savior: For history has always seen and will always see Christlike men and women of any faith or conviction unable to abandon their brothers and sisters. Because of them it is impossible to despair of humanity, and the world becomes habitable. Through them the suffering but saving God of Jesus is written in the passions of our daily life.

When we suffer, God-Crucified is our sorrow and God-Savior comforts us. When we serve, God-Crucified is the one we care for and God-Compassion is our action. If we sin, God is crucified in our heart, denying love, and God-Mercy is in our repentance. So repressed and forbidden, or caring and serving, or hurt and suffering, Love, God's presence in us, is always there, now. The Passion of Jesus is our daily bread in each one of us, in each of our days of denial, or crucifixion, or victory over evil (Is 49:1–6). The Passion of Jesus opens the gates to Hope.

In *The Grapes Of Wrath*, John Steinbeck expresses this

insight in a way I'll borrow here. Tom, the hero, is about to leave his mother. She asks, "How'm I gonna know 'bout you?" Often we wonder the same thing about God. But Tom's answer is like God's words written in our history since Jesus' Passion:

> Then I'll be all aroun' in the dark. I'll be ever'where— wherever you look. Wherever they's a fight so hungry people can eat, I'll be there. Wherever they's a cop beatin' up a guy, I'll be there.... I'll be in the way guys yell when the're mad an' — I'll be in the way kids laugh when they're hungry an' they know supper's ready. An' when our folks eat the stuff they raise an' live in the houses they build—why, I'll be there.*

---

*New York: Penguin Books, 1984, p. 463.

All Saved

Watchpeople in Vigil

I N THE PRECEDING CHAPTER WE spoke abundantly about
people who act for their suffering brothers and sisters.
What about the ones who cannot do anything directly
about the passion of their contemporaries? Right now,
what can I do for *each* country where there is a war or starvation, economic crisis or dictatorship, racism or misery,
child prostitution or slavery? What can I do for two friends
of mine, thirty-one and thirty-seven years old, who are dying from cancerous brain tumors? Sure, I can write checks
for humanitarian organizations, call politicians, send a
friendly card, support my friends' families. But I cannot
do anything directly. Who has not savored the bitterness
of such powerlessness? I can, however, always pray and
intercede.

Many people do, and no one should laugh at them because it shows that they take seriously into account the
sorrowful Passion of someone or some people, no less than
God does. Nothing there is trivial — neither the sufferings
and the dignity of the ones who hurt nor the concern and
care of the interceding people nor God's love for the needy
and the praying persons. The Scriptures are full of people
who interceded. John says that Jesus finished his last supper by interceding for his disciples and for us, and that he
still intercedes, as our "advocate with the Father"; so why

shouldn't we (Jn 17:9–23; 1 Jn 1:1; Rom 8:34)? He himself said that the days of ordeal for Jerusalem would "be shortened for the sake of the elect"; why would we not expect the same efficient grace for the days of any human ordeal if the elect intercede (Mt 24:22; Mk 13:20)? If Jesus' prayer was effective, why wouldn't ours be also, since we are indwelt by the Spirit who "intercedes" within us? (Rom 8:26–27). One thing is certain, if we believe the message of Exodus about Moses: When intercession stops, things get worse, and when it continues, things get better. For "as long as [Moses] kept his hands raised up, Israel had the better of the fight" against Amalek, and "when he let his hands rest, Amalek had the better of the fight" (Ex 17:8–13).

But we are not as great as Moses, Jesus, or the faithful elect, and we often intercede only when what occurs hurts *us*. So what could be the value of our intercession? Yes, we are not always concerned by the agony of a neighbor, a few blocks away from us, and we are frequently selfish petitioners. We must accept realistically and humbly that the world affects us only when it touches our own world. But for God it is better to hear our selfish intercession than to hear nothing at all. So whether we are able to act directly or not on a sorrowful situation, we must intercede and believe that God welcomes that, and we must trust the efficacy of our intercession.

It is already efficacious in terms of love in the one who intercedes. For as soon as our heart intercedes love in us wakes up and starts winning, because our carelessness and indifference are already gone. At last, our spirit joins the Spirit of Love who intercedes "with inexpressible groanings" within us (Rom 8:16, 26). But are we always really one with God's Spirit, especially when our powerlessness makes intercession extremely painful? Often we are torn by ambivalence: We would like to vent our frustration and anger but we also want to put these feelings aside and just care for our beloved one; we would like to escape and forget the ordeal, and yet we want to keep our heart constantly in vigil. Indeed, we are one with God, but with the Love we see in Jesus agonizing. We are efficacious when we intercede like this, as Jesus was in his agony. Though torn apart, we allow God-Love to save us from not loving. Intercessors, we are *saved* too.

Lest God should be appalled "that there was none to intercede," we must be Esther begging for her people and say, "Please God, take care of the one[s] I entrust to you. Give strength and determination, patience and discernment to the ones acting for good in the battlefield. Inspire more people to dare to join" (Est 5; Is 59:16). Furthermore, we must accept Jesus' invitation, "Pray for those who persecute you," and plead, "Soften the hearts of the ones who are hardened" (Mt 5:44). We must even say, "Forgive all of us because we do not know what we do." And because our faith guarantees that God is already active and such a prayer pleases the heart of the God of Jesus' Passion, we must believe that *all* will be saved, *all* "shall be well" (Julian of Norwich).

Finally, we must intercede, because if we don't, we'll lose out on a very special intimacy with God.

I will use Trinitarian language to explain this last point. When we allow the Spirit to intercede in us, we become a new prayer of the Son to the Father. Some would say that intercession is no longer necessary, especially when we believe that the Father already knows the cry of our heart and does not wait for our articulation in order to respond. That's just what I told a friend of mine years ago. She replied, "Yes, I know that. But I love to intercede for people because it gives *me* joy, and probably joy to God too." She was right. When we intercede we give the Spirit of the Son alive in us the joy of telling the Father about our care and concern for the one we pray for. Such a request gives the Father joy because he already loves the one we are holding before him (Jn 16:27). Of course this may be a painful joy because the one we are praying about is in pain, but it is

the joy shared by those who converse about someone they
both love who is suffering. It's as simple and beautiful as a
dialogue I heard one day:

> *The son of Mary and John was very sick. Mary had
> to leave home for a while. At the door, she said to
> her husband, "Please, take care of him." She already
> knew the reply, "Of course, I will." Unnecessary in-
> tercession? Somehow, yes. However, both were saying
> to each other how much, though painfully, they loved
> their child.*

Here we are talking about an intercession where God is
talking with God about the same Love, the same sorrowful
and loving Passion.

People who intercede write into history the same office that is written by contemplatives, who are always
keeping vigil for us before God. In that vigil, intercessors are burning with loving solicitude for others like can-
dles that can't be extinguished, and they remind us of
ourselves when we watch beside a sick child or a dying
spouse. Who would claim that these hours are wasted? In
fact, they are hours spent loving intensely, hours of love's
victory. People who watch are, in our blood and flesh,
an echo of Jesus' everlasting intercession before God that
Paul spoke about (Rom 8:34). They are like the crowds
who march in silent protest, apparently ineffective, but
we know what impact they have on public opinion and
on governments. The march of the mothers and wives of
the missing, "The Mothers of the Plaza de Mayo," every
Thursday in front of the government building, during the
years of the Argentinian military dictatorship (1976–83),
was one of the most striking examples of this kind of
demonstration. Who would dare say that these women
were ineffectual?

They "march" before the face of God like Hosea in
the image of paradise depicted in the play *Green Pastures.*
The unceasing repetition of their intercession echoes those

who, in their Passion, cry out for God, just like the pacing back and forth of the prophet before the door of God's office echoes the besieged warriors of Jerusalem. It is a call for God's grace, for a victory. And Love cannot remain indifferent.

GABRIEL: I hates to see you feelin' like dis, Lawd.

GOD: Dat's all right. Even bein' Gawd ain't a bed of roses (GABRIEL *exits.* HOSEA's *shadow is on the wall. For a second* HOSEA *hesitates.* GOD *looks at the wall. Goes to window*) I hear you. I know yo' fightin' bravely, but I ain't comin' down. Oh, why don' you leave me alone? You know you ain't talkin' to me. *Is* you talkin' to me? I cain't stand yo' talkin' dat way. I kin only hear part of what yo' sayin', and it puzzles me. Don' you know you cain't puzzle God? (*A pause. Then tenderly*) Do you want me to come down dere ve'y much? You know I said I wouldn't come down? (*Fiercely*) Why don' he answer me a little? (*With clenched fists, looks down through the window*) Listen! I'll tel you what I'll do. I ain't goin' to promise you anythin', and I ain't goin' to do nothin' to help you. I'm jest feelin' a little low, and I'm only comin' down to make myself feel a little better, dat's all.*

And, according to the play, God went down to Jerusalem and met one of the warriors, Hezdrel. God heard him talk about Hosea's God, a God full of the mercy discovered by the prophet himself "through sufferin'." And God understood... "dat even God must suffer." A friend of mine said to me, "I will never care for a God who does not suffer." God did. And when God accepted to suffer in Jesus' Passion, God was saved too.

---

*From Marc Connelly, in *Twenty Best Plays of the Modern American Theater* (New York: Crown Publishers, 1963), part 2, scenes 6 and 8, pp. 228–31.

God's Ordeal and Salvation

The Passion is also a grace for God, because in it there is written something entirely new and different about God.

The Passion of Jesus authenticates his words about God. In the Passion we perceive a God who is not indifferent but "at work until now" for us (Jn 5:17). "Sent not to condemn the world but to save it," Jesus shows there that God never condemns us (Jn 3:17; 12:47). Always in search of the lost sheep, this God cannot reject us, and says to us, "I *do* will it. Be cured" (Mt 18:12; Mk 1:41). "Our infirmities and sufferings" are borne personally by this God who is no longer a stranger to our sorrow (Mt 8:17). So that nothing "should be lost... but raised up on the last day," in order that we "might have life and life to the full," God, like the Good Shepherd, "gives his life for his sheep" (Jn 6:39; 10:10, 15). This is a God who wishes that we never hunger and thirst and that we be there where Jesus is — where "He will wipe every tear from [our] eyes, and there shall be no more death or mourning, wailing or pain, [for] the old order has passed away" (Jn 6:35; 14:3; Rv 7:16–17; 21:4).

In short, this is a God who, in the Passion of the man of Nazareth, obeys perfectly the commandments, "You shall love with your whole heart, with your whole soul, with your whole mind... You shall love your neighbor as yourself" (Mt 22:37). And this loving God is not a ghost, but our companion on the way through all the storms of our lives, and tells us, over and over: "It is I. Do not be afraid" (Mk 6:50).

And here is the grace of the Passion for God: In the crucified Jesus, we discover a God we can be attracted by, because it is *a God we can no longer fear* (Jn 8:28; 12:32; Mt 5:15).

History has seen God frequently misrepresented and disfigured, betrayed and dishonored by religious people. "Because of you the name of God is reviled among the

Gentiles," Paul reproached the Jews (Rom 2:24). Because of believers and their leaders, God's name became the one of a Judge, arbitrary and punishing pitilessly, the one of an Almighty beside the powerful and the rich, the one of a Creator and Ruler of the Universe indifferent and distant or dictating decrees without compassion. In God's name exclusions and racism, wars and genocides, persecutions and mass murders have been justified. Many false Messiahs have damaged and destroyed in a lot of people the true face of God (Mt 24:24). One recent example: After the disaster of Waco, Texas — where the guru David Koresh died with some followers and children — I wonder how many people have denied God a place in their existence?

Even within ourselves God has been victimized. Abusive parents and child molesters, some teachers and some ordained ministers, engraved in our subconscious a terrible picture of grownup persons, including God, when we were very young. God, as Love, could not be credible for years and years, if ever. And later, the bad examples of many Christians in all fields of life just reinforced the features of such a God. God could only be the object of fear and terror, disgust and hatred. Don't we suffer when our love is misunderstood? So did God, very probably, who said, "They hated me for no reason," and "O my people, what have I done to you? In what way have I wearied you? Answer me" (Jn 15:25; Ps 35:19; Mi 6:3). The French philosopher Voltaire once said, "God made man in his own image. Man got even with Him." Indeed, and we know that God is perfect Love!

Even in many religious writings, including some pages of the Old Testament (Lamentations, for instance), we still find a terrible God. Some trace of this carries over even into the New Testament, as we see in the terrifying story of Ananias and Sapphira (Acts 5:1–11). If we take such texts literally, with no sense of their historical context and correct purpose, God is horrible. But we easily buy such awful images of God because they trigger within us deadly unconscious impulses or conscious gluttony for power and exploitation. But Paul denies to all those forces, "principalities, powers," the capacity to separate us from the God revealed in Jesus' Passion (Rom 8:38–39). And he says, "It is precisely in this that God proves his love for us; that while we were still sinners, Christ died for us. Now that we have been justified by his blood, it is all the more certain that we shall be saved by him from God's wrath" (Rom 5:8–9; Is 55:13).

So God needed and still needs to be declared innocent of all our subconscious projections, and also of the distortions we create to justify our sins and our fanatical oppressions of others. It would be good to imitate Israel: Throughout the Old Testament, when something went wrong, they always thought that it could not be God's fault; it could be only theirs or the nations'. If we have contemplated the God revealed through Jesus in his Passion, we can eventually treat God as God, as Love. To some first Christians who were probably still afraid of God, John, following Paul, asserts, "Love has no room for fear; rather, perfect love casts out all fear" (1 Jn 4:18). If Jesus' Passion liberates us from the fear of God, it liberates also God-Love from our fear.

Thus, *God, who deserved it, is saved.*

It's up to us now to give this God-Passion the grace to exist in all of our daily Passions, Passions of suffering and Passions of service. "Begin the work!" said God through Haggai (Hg 2:4). Paul invites us to imitate him, "Forgetting what lies behind but straining forward to what lies ahead" (Phil 3:13–14, 17). God's seed grows inexorably, often painfully, always lovingly, but it is our honor to help it to do so (Mt 13:31–33; Is 55:10–11). That is God's life, that is our life, for it is the Passion of God *and* the Passion of our life. And, if we cannot act directly, we can still work through our Passions of intercession. If we do so, if we "help carry one another's burdens," we'll help God to achieve a last victory of the Passion, the one over oblivion. No longer will humankind be able to say, "We see no signs, no prophet any more" (Gal 6:2; Ps 74:9). "If I forget you, Jerusalem, may my right hand be forgotten! May my tongue cleave to my palate if I remember you not," sang the psalmist in exile (Ps 137:5–6). May we never forget the crucified ones — we have forgotten, for instance, people of Timor, that island near Australia that was invaded by Indonesia when it was no longer a Portuguese colony (1976). May we never forget the God of the crucified Jesus, may we be witnesses of Love. For that, we may say to God the words of a patient of a psychiatric institution to a friend of mine who supported him in his passion, till his death:

"Je me laisserai guider par votre singulière faculté
à vous dissoudre en m'apportant le réconfort."*

"I'll let myself be guided by your peculiar aptitude
to dissolve yourself through comforting me."

*Clément Porre, *Lettres à Michèle Reverbel*, Seyssel, France: Editions Comp'Act, France, 1992.

Scripture Index

Because they occur so frequently, citations from the accounts of the Passion in the four Gospels are not included here (Mt 26–27, Mk 14–15, Lk 22–23, Jn 18–19).

OLD TESTAMENT

NEW TESTAMENT

May I Hate God. New York: Paulist Press, 1979. 76 pages.

This book complements *God's Passion, Our Passion,* for those who may feel resentment and even hatred toward God because of what they are suffering or have suffered in their lives. Most of us have never been adequately taught how to manage these types of feelings with both intelligence and faith. *May I Hate God?* suggests one way in which these emotions will not go to waste.

Is God Deaf? Cambridge, MA: Cowley Publications, 1991. 115 pages.

Is this not one of our main questions when we suffer? This book shows that God is not deaf and that often we are the ones who cover our ears. It also recommends a way of praying that allows us to become aware of what we frequently refuse to hear.

Discernment, The Art of Choosing Well. Liguori, MO: Triumph Books, 1993. 145 pages.

We suffer when we do not know how to make a choice with God. Grounded in the spirituality of an expert in discernment according to the Christian tradition, this book unfolds in a systematic and simple way the stages of making a choice, whether that choice be by an individual or a group.